The bedroom offers part 2

The trend story, The bedroom offer

Joyce Brown

Table of Contents

Chapter 1

"What are you insinuating by you have no idea where all my money went?" I screamed banging the files on the table.

"It just vanished, totally untraceable"

"T hired an incompetent ACcountant" l yelled
at him

"I'm sorry sir"

"Will sorry bring back my funds?"

"All our investors withdrew their funds so we are left with just Mr. Johnson who is likely to pull out as well" my secretary informed me and that only infuriated me the most.

"We need investors so, place the company shares with discount"

"The issue is that no one is willing to buy shares from us"

"What?"

"Sir at this rate we are going bankrupt"

"This can't be happening. What about the loan we got from the bank how do I pay

it back? The collateral was this company and I have just one month to pay back
"Sir we still got one investor we just..."
Just then Mr. Johnson came into my office.
"Ah Mr. Johnson I wasn't expecting
you"
"I came here for something urgent I just found a bigger deal and I need to withdraw my funds".
"Mr. Johnson we can talk about this. You don't have to withdraw because I will offer you a better deal"
"Your company is at the peak of bankruptcy and you have nothing to offer. Just get me my money and stop delaying me"
"Mr. Johnson, can we talk this out? we have been business associates for years so I beg for reconsideration".
"This is business Kennedy and there is no permanent friend. You see a bigger deal you go for it can't keep wasting my funds on a a business that is no longer profitable"
"But "
"No buts just give me my money and stop

wasting my time"
"Transfer all his funds back to him"
"Just a minute" My accountant operating
"You got your money, sign the damn papers and leave my office" I told him when he received the alert.
He signs the paper and stands up to leave.
"Before I leave Mr. Kennedy I have a word for you. The people that are fighting against you are way bigger than you" he said and walked out of my office.
"Bigger than me?" Could this be revenge? Could Gold be the one behind this? No way, she left just weeks ago, how could she be fighting me?
But her father and his family disappeared all of a sudden, could she possibly be protecting them too?
How can that be? Where did she acquire the such amount of money to fight me? No, it
can't be Gold she can't be back to take revenge. I will kill her if she does.
properties and put it back into the business.

It's just like starting over from scratch, I'm gonna make the person behind
this pay.
ETHAN
"Everything was going according to plan. Kennedy will soon go bankrupt.."l smiled as he said that. He wouldn't know what strikes him.
Phase two is making sure he never rises, you don't want to know what I got in stock for him in phase three. When I'm through him, he will learn to keep his dick in his pants.
"He also took a loan some months ago and used his company as collateral"
"That's even better I'm not giving him a chance to rise. How much longer does he have to pay back"

"One month”

"One month is just too long have the bank speed it up to a week. Right now, he would be thinking of selling his properties to raise funds for his business. All the buyers will be sent by me so when he gets his money, he would put it back into his business. That's where his accountant will come in handy again diverting his funds and running away"

"He will get the biggest shock when the the bank will give him a week to pay off his debts. He would never be able to meet it and before his very eyes, his company will be gone"

"Fredrick you are a guru seems like you already have everything planned out. I just hope it works out as planned"

"lt will it's like starting all over he will therefore need to sell off his properties, rent a smaller place and cut off his expenses. I didn't become a businessman for nothing its simple business logic"

a fun-filled night brother" he smiled and left my room.
"I sure will" | smiled.
GOLD
My heart was beating at a rapid rate as I halted in front of his door still deciphering whether to go in or not.
I was on a white spa robe and wasn't putting on any underwear. My feet had on them a simple slippers and my hair fell freely and it smelt of the strawberry
the shampoo I used.
It was all Ella's idea she said a robe will be easier to pull off and she suggested not wearing any inner wears.
"Are you going to come in or not?" I heard his voice. How did he know I'm out here?
I slowly opened the door and closed the door behind me. He was just on simplc trousers and was bare-chested so, I couldn't help but admire him

"Are you just going to stand there staring at me or will you come over? just kept playing with the hem of my robe. and he walked up to me pinning me against the door. I felt myself slowly losing my breath as his eyes stared into mine.
Slowly he took my lips in his and transported me to cloud nine.
I kissed him back and wrapped my hands around his shoulders.
The kiss grew hotter and aggressive and I Wrapped my legs around him. He carried me and dropped D me on the bed as I looked
into his eyes breathing heavily as his hands fiddle with the cincture of my robe before losing it entirely.
His eyes were filled with desires as he stared at my body.
"You are beautiful Gold," he says as he slowly took one of my hard nipples in his mouth and moaned softly as he socked on

my nipples giving it soft bites.
"Allow me to make you feel like a woman Gold" he whisper as his hands move to my core. I gasp and parted my legs open for him because I wanted him so much now.
"Yes please,"l moaned as two of his fingers slid into me. His lips sucked on my nipples as his fingers worked on my core.
My body flatter as I moan meeting he he he the the the the thrust of his fingers.It felt so good, no one
has ever made me feel this way before.
I moaned out loudly as my body twitched violently. His legs pinned me further into the bed as my orgasm broke. I felt warm liquid spurt out of me as my moans reduced.
His fingers slide in and out of me and i watched him take off his trousers.
I gasped slightly seeing his enormous length. He smiled seeing my reaction.
"Like what you see?" he asked smiling and I

nodded shyly.
He slowly directed his length to my entrance and penetrated me slowly and I let out a loud moan. He groaned as my core adjusted to his length.
He takes it out of me again and slides it back in earning another moan from my mouth.
Slowly he increased his pace thrusting into me at a faster pace. My legs hung on his shoulders and my ass bounced to his thrust "This feels so good...oh my God" I moaned digging my fingers into his back. I could feel my orgasm building up inside of me. My moans were enough to shake the whole mansion.
I couldn't take it anymore as I moaned loudly having another mind-blowing orgasm I felt my core tighten around him as he moaned.
"Shit. I'm gonna moan driving into me with full force as our skin slapped against each other as my moans became louder again.

I was so close and I could feel another orgasm on the way. We both exploded together as my core milked all his cum. His length slide out of me as he lays beside me and cuddled me in his arms and | smiled. That was great.

FLORENCE

I walked into the kitchen and met three maids talking.

"You hear the way she
screamed last night"

"| think the master didn't go easy on her at all"

"Seems like she'll conceive a child for him after all"

""Yes I think the master loves her a lot and he may end up getting married to her"

I got angry from hearing their conversation and walked out of the kitchen thinking of ways to deal with Gold.

"Don't try to toucha touch an of her hair Florence the master would end up your chopping your head off" Ella snmiledsmiledg me off the way.

"Don't say I didn't warn you"she scowls at me and walked into the kitchen.
I must have the master by any means necessary I'll never loose to Gold Never.
I opened my eyes and saw my master's handsome face staring at me. I grinned recalling all that happened last night.
"Good morning"
"Stop staring at me like that"l sulked and he smiled climbing on top of me.
"Why shouldn't I?" he said rubbing his
my life"
"Your mom was a treasure to you"
"Yes she was my anchor but when she died, my whole world crumbled. I had to stay strong like she said, at times, I wished she were still alive then my life wouldn't have been complicated especially when I thought I could live then | was abused" it hurts badly.
"I'm sorry Gold but I'm here now and I won't
let anyone hurt you
"I trust you Fredrick. AMyfoster

father sold me out to make life difficult for me but on the contrary, he blessed me instead as you came to me as a guardian anAngel"I want to give you a taste of my world"
"Really?"
"Yes darling i will take you out tomorrow and let the whole world know that you are mine"

"I'd love that"
EMMANUELLA
"What? he seriously asked you to be his girlfriend?"
"Yeah"
"That's great news soon it will be baby alert" she giggled and I smiled.
"'Seriously? Gold the master has been fucking you from last night till this morning"
Ella said and I blushed.
"You are even smiling i thought you said you weren't going yesterday.Your moans were disturbing my sleep"

"Daniela" T hit her shoulders playfully.
"But it's true you know I have so many cute baby names"
"Celebrating your victory right?" Florence said walking to us.
"Don't you get tired?" I asked crossing my arms.
"I don't. The master is mine but you seduced your way into his bed. I will get what belongs to me. Mark my words Gold i will make you pay
"You wont do nothing Florence you are just a jealous bitch" Ella retorted.
"Watch your back Gold because I'm coming for you" She gave me a dangerous look and walked away.
"How dare you?" Ella proceed to attack her but I held her back.
"Let me deal with this bitch"
"L,et her go Ella, she's the least of my problems now"
"Sometimes I think you're too easy-going"
"Just let her be I don't want her to ruin our mood"

"If you say so. So did you give him:
BJ?
"Emmanuella???"
"What?"
"Never mind. You are too holy for that's grinned.
"Whatever"
ETHAN
"I knew you liked her all along. You were just pretending" I smiled as he said that.
"You even smile now. She did
wonders to you"
"Stop it will you?"
"Noi won't.
"Let's just talk about something else. How's my revenge plan coming up?"
"We are on point. Your plan worked wonders and he's already ruined"
"Suspend the idea about giving his money to his son. I won't
offer him any chance to recover. Despite the fact that his father is evil, he might ask for help or the father might get suspicious of his son"

"You're right you know. So you are bringing her to the annual successful C.E.o's party"
"Yeah I've never taken any girl with me before"
"That's because you've never gotten really serious with any girl".
"I did have a highschool girlfriend dummy"
"We both know you were just playing around"
"Ethan I have work to do" I told him facing my computer screen signifying the end of our disCussion.
KENNEDY
"What do you mean he disappeared with my money?" I grab hold of her neck.
"'Sir I can't breathe" she said trying to catch
"But I have one month to pay"
"Not anymore you have just a week Mr Kennedy.
Good day one of the guys dropped a notice paper on the table.
I sank into my chair hopeless. I'm doomed.
GOLD
I smiled satisfactorily at my reflection in the

mirror. I wore a black mini dress that revealed my curves and round ass. It also had a slit that left the side of my lap slightly exposed.
I wore a red pair of stilettoes heels with a beautiful jewelry set adorned on my neck, ears and wrist with my brown long hair falling freely against my back.
Fredrick actually took me out for shopping and he also got me a new phone.
"Oh my God Gold you look beautiful. The master will drool when he sees you in this Outfit"
"You're crazy I'm off Ella take care"l kissed her cheek.
"Have fun bestie"she giggled as I walked out of the room. Nicholas was outside ready to escort me to meet Fredrick who was patiently waiting for mc at thc parking lot.
"Gold, this dress looks really perfect on you" Fredrick commented looking at me in amazement.
"Thanks"l replied shyly and got into the car

with him seating next to me while Nicholas sat at infront with the driver. I guess Ethan will be using the other car.
The driver started the engine as the car zoomed off.
We walk into the party holding hands as hip hop music blast out of the speakers.
People could be seen dancing and they all looked smelt of wealth.
"Fredrickson girl ran to hug him almost knocking me off but he held tight to my hands.
"Joy, what are you doing here?"'he inquired getting her off me. I can't believe she's attempting to flirt with my man. I became angry but I decided to keep my cool.
"Ain't you happy to see me?"
"Listen, what we had back then inthe high school wasn't anything so don't allow it dominate your head"
"But Fredrick'she turned and stared at me, giving me a bad look.
"So who is this?"
"My fiancee"

"Your girlfriend? What about me? Are you going to dump me for this thing"
"Don't call my girlfriend names besides we broke up a long time ago so stop making a Scene"
"Frederick I feel tired and sleepy can you please take me home?"l asked getting bored by her incessant ranting.
"Of course darling'"
"Fredrick'she called but we walked away then I turned and rolled my tongue at her before leaving.
"On getting outside a lot of reporters bombarded us with loads of questions as they also took pictures of us.
"M.r Fredrick who is this beautiful lady with you?"
"She is my fiancee"
"She must be really lucky to havc you've both smiled as a reporter said that.
"Of course she is"
"What's the name of the beauty who put a smile on M.r Fredrick's face?"
"Gold MamaCollins'sl replied smiling and

his hands secured my waist kissing me slightly.
Awwn they look so cute together"
"That will be enough questions now"
Nicholas and Chike helped us walk through the crowd of paparazzi. I guess I'm officially a celebrity now.
KENNEDY
"Dad what are you doing here?"Caleb asked as l entered his room.
"I came to see you my son Is that a problem
"Yes because I can't have a monster as a father"
"Watch your tongue Caleb"
"You murdered my mum and hid it from me for a long time, made me take advantage of my step sister, almost killed me from the sleeping drug overdose and so many evil things.You are more than demon's slap landed on my cheek and I held my face.

"I heard of the recent misfortune that came your way nemesis has finally caught up with you
"What do you mean?"
"Can't you see dad, Gold is back to hunt you
"That's impossible she's a wretched bitch"
"Wretched bitch you call her You sold her into slavery but you made her life better without knowing it's brought out his phone and showed me a picture of Gold kissing a guy.
He appeared wealthy and she was looking more beautiful.
"No this can't be.. it can't be"
"Your evil is back to hunt you and you can't run away from it.

Chapter 2

KENNEDY

I can't believe this, so Gold has been behind my misfortune allthise while. I was so stupid to see the handwriting on the wall, now I'm Not the verlosingoosing everything. Just one week to pay up my debts or my company will be confiscated. I will become poor and I hate being poor. Why would she only come after me? After all Caleb joined in raping her.

Scheap prostitute who went to look for some rich guy to spread her legs for. I need to look for a way to get money and end her life once and for all.

"She would regret ever toiling with me" I said tomef.

"You are still very unrepentant Instead of thinking of a way to apologize to her of which I know she would never forgive you. You proved me right by being the monster you are sometimes I wonder how I became your son"

"Don't you dare speak to me in such manner
because am still your father but you seem to have forgotten something Caleb We both had Gold that night so don't try to run away from it If I'm going down then I'm dragging you with me"

"You are a devil Dad Why can't you just letIe be?"

"We are both devils, she begged Caleb but you showed her no mercy now tell me you didn't like her tiny little pussy"

"'Stop it and leave my room now he yelled.

"You can't run away from it Caleb cause it's the truth and you are being hunted by the truth"

"l apologized and she forgivc mc so don't try to drag me into your mess"

"My mess you say what makes you think did she forgive you? You were so stupid to

have believed her"
"I made a stupid mistake and l apologized cause I had a conscience but what did you do? You treated her like garbage, maltreated the daughter of the woman you claimed to lov,e and sold her into slavery. You are worst than the devil and I've got something you can never have a conscience. That's what evil souls like you don't have "he yelled.
He left me dumbfounded with his words e has never spoken to me that way before.
"As you can see the door is wide open. Get out of my room. one more thing, don't try to harm Gold. You might end up killing yourself in the process wat amIi even saying you can do nothing, you don't have any money so enjoy being poor you deserve death"
"Caleb"
"Get out and never come back"

"I will be back said walking out of the room.
"When next we see I hope to see you in acoffine yelled slamming the door at my face.
"lt is Gold that would be in a coffin"I retorted before leaving his door post.I need to look for a way to kill her and I will be needing a lot of money.

FREDRICK

"Who was that?"She asked when we got into the car.
"My ex-girlfriend she shouldn't be a bother to you'll smiled at her as she rested her head on my shoulders.
"I hope she wont she muttered and I think she slept off.
I stoked her hair gently admiring her beautiful face.
"l can't believe you are mine now"l

whispered kissing her forehead softly.
GOLD
My eyes parted open slowly as I sat up stretching myself on the bed.
"Up already?" I turned to see Fredrick already dressed in a black suit ready to go the work. I checked the wall clock and it was already a few minutes past eight.
"Yeah and how come I woke up late,," I asked
walking to him.
"You slept late.I guess"l nodded and helped him
knot his tie.
"I'm off" he smiled and pulled me into a short kiss.
"What about breakfast?"
"l guess I will skip that I have an important board meeting to attend and I'm running late"
"Ok don't stay out too late"

"I won't" then he pulls me into another kiss before leaving.
I sigh and headed to the bathroom to freshen up.
After bathing,l came out of bathroom with my towel wrapped around my body, I applied my body lotion to my skin wore my a T-shirtT-shirtT-shirts before going out.
An idea popped into my head and I smiled to myself.
"I so much like this idea of yours"Ella giggled as we walked to the kitchen plankitchening fried rice and chicken for Fredrick.
"Where do you guys think you are going?" seeing Florence almost made me throw up. i despise her guts too.
"I don't have time for the trash you want to says he held my arms as I prOceed to walk out.
"Let me go bitch"l screamed and pu her off

and she landed her buttocks on the ground.
"That serves you right Ella rolled her tongue out mockingly as we walked away.
Getting into the kitchen, we met Amara
"Hey Amara"
"Hi Gold'she smiled.
"So I'l be needing your help on something"
"You are the master's girlfriend now. Helping you is like helping the master"
"That's nice of you'
They both helped me out with the preparation of the food. I did most of the cooking though they just assisted in speeding up things.When I finished the food, i cut the pizza into slices using a pizza cutter and put it in a pizza carton box. The fried rice was served in a medium sized thermo food flask along with some fried chicken at the top of the food.

"Thanks alot for this"l smiled at both of them who were busy eating the other pizza we made.
"You are welcome"
"Gold you look all sweety go and freshen up and dress sexy'Ella giggled and I also took a bite from the pizza it tasted nice.
Of course I will"
"Let's gorilla carried the food basket and followed me to my room.
"Of course, I will"
"Let's go' Ella carried the food basket and followed me to my room.I had my bath and dressed in a white jump suit and a white boot heels.
I wore an earring with a necklace and Ella helped me apply light make up to my face I smiled at my appearance in the mirror.
"Gold you look breathtaking hc master

pop
might end up eating you along with the food
"Geez Ella"
"Whatever let me go tell Nicholas to prepare the car for you"
"Ok"
The drive to his office was quite a long one. | sat at the rear while Nicholas sat at the passengers seat and of course thethe the chauffeur was at the drivers seat.
I looked outside of the tinted glass window watching the hustles and bustles of the city. Lagos sure is beautiful with so many magnificent buildings.The car finally halted at a beautiful high rise building that had inscription boldly written 'Majestic Corporation'.
I stepped down elegantly as my heels touched the ground Nicholas offered to carry the basket for me and | let him besides its quite heavy.

As I walked into the building the workers stared at me in awe as they muttered to themselves.

I walked to the receptionist and smiled at her.

"Hi, how may I help you?"

"Im here for my boyfriend Fredrick Majesty your boss"

"Wow I didn't know it was you. Just take an elevator to the top floor, you will know he's office when you get there. He's actually less busy now"

"Ok thanks"l smiled at her before walking to the elevator. The elevator ride took a few minutes and the door binged as it slide open.

Walking out of the elevator I sighted a woman right outside the door with a tag C.E .o's office.

"Who are you?"

"Gold, i came to see my boyfriend Fredrick"

"You are his girlfriend?"she asked looking at me from head to toe.

"Yes She gave my scornful stares

"The boss is in a meeting"

"What do you mean the receptionist said he less busy"

"Are you deaf or have you suddenly Iost your senses?"

"Hey watch your tongue young lady" Nicholas said.

"Tell her to watch it too now leave and when the boss is less busy you can come"

"Are you insane?"| asked cause she was ranting like a mad person to me.

"It is you that is insane you whore"

Just then, Fredrick walked out of the office angry probably because of the noise. I can't

believe she called me a whore and I'll make sure she pays for that word.
"Gold"his eyes softened seeing me then he pulled me into a short kiss and then turned to his rude secretary who was already shivering from anxiety.
"What was going on here?"
"Boss ... I...'she stammered.
"She called me a whore because i wanted to see you"
"What? You called my girlfriend a whore?"'he
sounded really furious.
"Sir l'm sorry... I ..'she went on her knees begging in tears.
"Get out of my Company You are fired"...

Chapter 3

"Master Fredrick, I'm sorry this is my only means of survival"
"You should have reflected about that before calling my Fiancee names"I wanted talking to Fredrick about letting her go but then she still gave me scornful glances when she felt Fredrick wasn't looking.
He sighted her when she did that and it provoked him the more.
"Michael"
"Yes boss"
Get this piece of trash out of my premises
"Boss, please you can't fire me" she yelled crying as Michael carried her out.
"Let go me you fool" she shouted struggling with him and I sighed when they were out of sight.
"l'm sorry about that my treasure" Fredrick said to me as we approached his office.
"lit's very glaring that she's into you' I sighed

"Don't be jealous?" he smiled relaxing on the couch.
"Is there a reason why I shouldn't? moreover
, I'm your fiancee" I frowned my face and sat on his laps while he laughed.
"She should be the least of your problems moreover I'm yours now" I smiled when he said that.
"Baby, I love you but your admirers are massive. I'm afraid they will attempt to harm me."
"No one will dare harm you Gold and anyone who does, I will kill and I mean it".
"Fred, thank you for coming into my life"
His hands grabbed my cheeks affectionately. "I love you Gold"
I smiled tearfully because i never thought of meeting a person like Fredrick who would love me sincerely and unconditionally.
I'm the most luckiest woman on earth to have a man like him in my life. He brought

joy into my life and I would be a liar to say I don't love him too.

"| love you Fred" his hands wipe off my tears as he crushed his lips against mine and I kissed him back wrapping my hands around his shoulders. He deepened the kiss as he brushed off the stands of hair on my face then he pulled out of the kiss staring at me intensely.

"Listen, I got something for you" immediately

"Fred, l'm here to apologize for insulting your fiancee the other day. You were correct after all that had was a child's play"

"I brought you this as a token of my apology I grinned as it replayed in my head thinking of how to make him eat the food I prepared. I smiled happily as I entered into his company building. I'm ovulating today so I intend giving him the food in wwhichoured sex pills to it.

He will certainly consume it and become

very horny and then he will make love to me oh how I've missed having him inside of me but after today, I will be carrying his child then, he will discard that bitch of a fiancee and go for me. Besides i can't let him slip away being with him is like winning a lottery so i really won't let him slip through my fingers and cling to that Gold girl or whatever or her name is.
I approached the receptionist with a fake smile.
"Welcome mam please what do you want?" she asked.
"Well l'm here I'msee your boss, my boyfriend *
"Excuse me but I think you are mistaken
"What do you mean I'm mistaken? my friend
take me to him now"
She unlocked her phone and placed the screen towards me and what i sighted almost gave me a heart failure.
"Popular business magnet Mr. Fredrick Majesty unveiled his beautiful fiancee, Miss

Gold Mama Collins to the world the news displayed and I sighted photographs of her smiling at the camera and also photographs of them kissing.
"So why did you show me this?" I inquired in
annoyance.
"Because I want to know how you look like her? quit assuming what you're not"
"'Save that address and tell me where I can find Fredrick?"
"In his office with his fiancee"
"Fiancee?" i muttered that bitch! how can i give Fredrick the food I prepared.
I decided to walk towards the elevator when I heard the receptionist said something.
"Ladies like you are the issues we have in this planet. scouting for other people's fiancee to grab"
Instantly, a lady was being dragged roughly by the guards and she kept shouting telling the guy to release her.
"Juliet, wetin happen?" the receptionist

asked smile a co-worker of hers.
"my dear, ignore her ooo she referred to Mr Fredrick's fiancee as a slut so the boss grew really mad and fired her"
"But that girl is so senseless. It's obvious that she likes the boss but to the level of insulting his fiancee, that's bad".
"Who wouldn't fall for the boss? he is wealthy and good looking. I envy that girl | just wish I were in her shoes"
"Stop thinking of the impossible madam It's glaring the boss adores her very much. Remember the way he defended her. but the lady appears like a nice person not all those gold diggers who are only chasing him because of money.
"Yes ooo She is and I need a man like that" Julie said.
"Don't mind some people trying to wreck a good relationship" the receptionist said giving me glares and I got really upset and left their presence to the elevator.
"'She better holds her man tight before

Someone else try to steal him the receptionist shouted lou me to hear. I fumed and went to the elevator punched the buttons on it and it closed. I alighted when I got to the first floor and went straight to the office that had the C.E.o's name and opened it angrily. Only to see her on his lap and they were both smiling about something and I saw that she had already set the table with the food she brought.This stupid girl just destroyed my plans of having Fredrick to myself.
"Fredrick I screamed and they turned to look at me.
"Joy, what are you doing here?" he asked and pecked Gold in front of me.
"What is this Gold digger doing here Joy asked?" but his countenance transformed into an angry one.
"If you ever refer to my fiancee as a good digger, again you won't like the out come of what I'|| do to you"
"Can't you see that I love you Fred, are you blind? end whatever it is that you have with

this girl she'll bring misfortune to us"
"Joy leave my office now before I call my men to beat you up"
"If she doesn't leave you alone thenI will hurt her badly"
"Then be prepared to die"
Fear dominated Gold when she said that so just rested her head on Fred's shoulders smirking perhaps enjoying the show although she was scared.
"What?"
"You heard me clearly leave my office"
"I will be back" you can't keep safeguarding her forever Frederick you must be mine. I will never loose you to her.
"Fred, Gold called him it's obvious am not wanted here so i think I should be on my way"
"But I want you here. Listen up baby those people are only envious of you because l didn't pick any of them so they should be the least of your problem"

"Ok"l nodded.
"I dislike seeing your face unhappy can you at least smile please" he beamed and tickled me and I laughed heartily.
"Fred, stop it "Gold laughed then he pulled her in for a brief kiss smiling and she reciprocated.
"Can you dish out my food already i'm starvIn "he complained grabbing his stomach and she laughed.
"I never knew you could be dramatic Gold smiled opening the food flask.
"the dramatic one is Ethan and not me"
"That reminds me where is he?"
"He went to supervise the factory... My God, this is so delicious. Did you prepare it yourself??"
"Yeah but Ella and Amara assisted "Gold said to him as she served the wine into glasses and rested on his lap.
He took a slice of the pizza and bites from it

"This taste good"
"Thanks. but I want you to eat the fried rice as well"
"Feed me"he pouted and I carried up the spoon, filled it with rice, and shoved it into his mouth. He smiled as he tasted the food
"This is also delicious butI can't eat all of it"
"That's why I'm here"
"T thinkl came in earlier for a reason Ethan smiled making his way to the office.
"Hello bro, I can see you are enjoying yourself. I think I should get my own girlfriend don't you think being single is a disease?".
He grabbed a slice of pizza and shoved it into his mouth. "Wow this taste delicious did you really prepare these?"
"Of course I did" then he carried another one.
"I hope you have no intention of consuming everything here?"

"Only if can, why not" he rolled his eyes.
"Bro, it will be sufficient for all of us"
He joined us in eating the food and went back home afterwards.
Ella and I talked about alot of things when I came back home. I feel sick all of a sudden and I had to throw up.
"Gold, are you ok?"
"Im fine"
"But you are turning blanch"
"I'm alright l just want to relax"
"Are you sure?"
"Yeah'l smiled mildly.
"Ok She led me to the bed and used the duvet to wrap me up before leaving the room. What's wrong with me? I feel powerless instantly so I closed my eyes gradually and darkness took over.
Frederick dismissed early from work because he wanted to see Gold. When he arrived home, he saw Ella coming out of his

room looking worried and he couldn't help but imagine what the issue was?
"Good evening master'she greeted.
"Where is Gold?"
"'She's in the room but I think she's not feeling fine"
"Sick?" He hurriedly went to the room and saw her on the bed with her eyes closed. She appeared lifeless but she was healthy this afternoon.
"Gold" he called but there was no response So he lifted her hands up and saw track marks on them.
"Poison?"
So he carried her on his arms out of the room with Ella following them behind.
Who has Gold offended that they attempt to kill her? l just hope she will be fine because will sure kill the person behind this.
at the waiting room still deep in thoughts praying she survives this, I love her so much and I can't live without her.

"Mr Fredrick" | heard the doctor's voice as he came out of the room.
"How is she faring?"l asked worried
"She's stable now the poison has already been destroyed but she is yet to revive. If she was delayed for 15 minutes before coming to the hospital, we may have lost her.
But i have an unpleasant announcement"
"Unpleasant?"
"Yes she was poisoned and because of that poison, the zygote in her fallopian tube washed away'
Are you trying to say that she conceived, please tell me how did it happen?"
"Well, her body came in contact with a lethal material"
"'Skin?"
"Yes the skin can absorb bàne substances into it and judging by the rate of the poison in her body, it was a slow poison so it means she was poisoned in the morning".

"'So the person who committed this executed it in the morning Fredrick inquired ?"
"Definitely Sir"
"Thank you Doctor so can i see her now?
"Of course you can if you'd excuse me, i have other patients to attend to"
"Ok"l sighed and entered the room. Seeing Gold in the hospital lying on the bed defence defenseless my heart.
I drew a chair beside her and grabbed her hands that looked lifeless. The fact that she was carrying my baby and some idiots had the nerves to do this to her, angered me to the highest.
I stayed back with her at the hospital all night watching her as she slept peacefully.
My eyes opened when I felt someone's touch on my hair. and when i stood up to see who it was, I spotted Gold grinning at me. I wiped my eyes to be sure that it wasn't a dream but she kept smiling at me.
She rolled her eyes at me "Fred you are not

dreaming lI'm awake she,.,.,.,. laughed and embraced her on the bed.
"Baby its not funny at all you scared me".
"Well I'm fine alright now so what happened to me?" she inquired petting my face romantically.
"You were poisoned"
"Poisoned?"
"The doctor said your skin connected with a toxic substance.
Baby, Fredrick called can you recall anyone touching you during morning hours?"
"My God, it's Florence that wicked girl, she touched my arms yesterday and I got upset and pushed her away so It's possible that she was the person who did that moreover, she's the only one who expresses hatred for me in the house"
"For attempting to kill you Gold she will die"
"Fredrick"
"Don't attempt to plead with me because I

won't even listen to you. I meant every Word I said at the office I should have finished her off when she first attempted to kill you"

"Come-on darling, I'm ok now."

"I know but she still needs to go. What if something terrible had happened to you?"

Immediately, the doctor walked into the ward accompanied by a nurse.

"Good morning Mr Fredrick"

"Good morning doctor" we shook hands.

"Miss Gold you are awake?" he asked surprised.

"Is there an issue with that?"

"Not at all. We just didn't expect her to revive so quickly" he said examining her while the nurse removed the syring on her hand.

"So does it mean I will leave now" she grinned.

"Not yet we still need to observe you for some days especially since you had.

Chapter 4

"How I came across it isn't necessary but trying to kill my fiancee is the biggest offense you can ever commit. I made an error by not taking you to the cold room the previous time you faltered but today I'll make sure you die there" Fredrick shouted at her.
"You can't kill me because of Gold, Florence said. If only you didn't get home early that nuisance of a fiancee would have been gone"
"I see you have the nerve? Nicholas, Fredrick called take this girl and discard her in the cold room"
"Yes Master" Nicholas carried her roughly on his shoulders and took her Out.
"Release me oh Gold I detest you"...She shouted as she was being taken out.
"Good riddance.
Joy knocked at the door and flashed a smile at Bianca who came to open it. She

used her fame and connections to acquire Bianca's house address.

"Yes who are you and how can I help you ?" Bianca asked staring at her.

"Can I come in"? Joy asked but Bianca stared at her suspiciously before letting her in. Her house looked really beautiful but it's so unfortunate that she will have to sell it if she doesn't get a decent job.

"May I?"

"Sure you can seat" I sat on the couch and she sat on the opposite couch.

"What brings you here? And who are you?"

"My name is Joy Martins and I'm here to help you. Joy answered beaming at her.

"I don't understand?"

"I heard you lost your job because of your boss's fiancee"

"Yes but what are you driving at?"

"Don't you want your boss and don't you want revenge?"

"I want no issues at all. My boss can be a dangerous man if provoked"

"Don't be a loser once she's out of the way you can have him all to yourself. I will give you all the money you need to ensure she dies"

"Why do you want to assist me?"

"You see that girl is evil, she took my husband away from me and after killing him, she absconded with his money and ran to be with Fredrick" I started crying being fully aware that she will fall for it.

"I'm sorry you experienced such"

"I'm only trying to help your boss because I don't want him to end up like my husband. I know he likes you but she must have used black magic to cast a spell on him"

"Yes I thought as much too because he loves her so much"

"So are you willing to get vengeance for us?"

"Yes I will do it" I smiled inwardly she's

so dewy-eyed
I'll only use her to achieve my plans and the moment I'm done with her, I will kill her. No body is entitled to share Fredrick with me not at all.
Ethan, Fredrick called his brother" I don't want Gold to get into more danger because of those girls hovering around me"
"So what do you intend to do?" Ethan asked
"I know Joy, she doesn't back down easily so I need eyes on her. Bianca my former the secretary might not be able to do anything because she's jobless but at the same time we never can tell if she has something coming up so I need someone to watch her as well. I won't give either of them the chance to get to me"
"Then as for Kennedy, I need him here, seeing Gold will make him talk thrash and spill out all the atrocity he has committed and It will be used as proof against him in court because I will

charge him to court with a death sentence for raping Gold, and killing Carol (Caleb's mum), attempted murder of Collins and finally for killing Irene (Gold's mum).

Chapter 5

"It's so good to be back here" Gold giggled as she walked into the room with Frederick.
"Yeah, I missed you being here as well" Fredrick said as he smiled sitting on the bed.
"Well I'm here now Gold said seating on his laps.
"I don't want to ever lose you Gold, I love you so much" Fredrick said.
"I love you too Darling and you are losilosingme"
"Gold, I have something to tell you" Fredrick said sounding serious.
"What is it?" Gold asked anxiously
"I know I should have told you this earlier but your dad was almost killed by gunmen some weeks ago" Fredrick said.
"What?" Gold asked getting up from his lap.
"Why tell me this now Fred? this is

my father, we are talking about" Gold said in a disappointed tone.
"Look I'm sorry babe for not telling you" he said and Gold felt his hands around her waist.
"I hate being kept being the dark so please don't hide things from me again" Gold warned.
"I promise that I won't but does it mean that you've forgiven me," Fredrick asked whispering against her neck and she bit her lips.
"Are you seriously going to seduce the forgiveness out of me" Gold asked as she turned to face him.
"If I have to then Yes "Fredrick smirked crushing his lips against hers and she kissed him back wrapping her hands around his neck as she also wrapped her legs around his torso.
The kiss got hotter and it was obvious that it was going to lead to sex then he pulled out of the kiss and looked at her.
"Why did you stop?" Gold asked as she

pouted.
"Gold, you just got back from the hospital and I don't think.." Frederick was about to make a statement but Gold shut him up with a kiss.
"I want you now Fredrick" She whispered in between kisses.
After rounds of intense love-making, Gold smiled to herself as he cuddled her in his arms and her hands rested on his a chest as she stared at him.
"Baby I've got something important to tell you" Fredrick said.
"What is it?" Gold asked again
"It's about Kennedy".
"Is he dead, If he is then I don't mind dropping thorns at his grave" Gold said huffing.
"He's not yet dead but he will very soon"
Gold looked at him with a different expression as he told her all he did to Kennedy.

Gold was thinking of a better revenge plan not knowing that Fredrick had already taken care of it.

"You did that for me?" Gold asked trying hard not to cry because she never for once thought she will find a man like Fredrick in her lifetime who loves and cares for her so much.

"He hurt you Gold, so I had to make him

"Freddie, I love you," Gold said as she hugged him tight on the bed.

"I love you more Goldie" Fredrick replied as he kisses her forehead.

"I's time for the final phase baby, It's time to charge him to court because his crimes are way too much I'm certain it will earn him a death sentence" Fredrick said.

"He deserves worse than death"

"Gold this may be sad to hear but he was the one who planned to kill your father and he also killed your mother" Fredrick said.

"What? Kennedy killed my mom, how is that was even possible when it was confirmed that she died of a stroke" Gold said
"Yeah she did but Kennedy paid the doctor to get the real hospital file not knowing that the doctor had another
In the file, your mom bleed because of a head injury and my guess is that Kennedy has something to do with that if not he wouldn't have asked the doctor to hide the real file" Fredrick said.
"Kennedy killed my mom? No wonder he buried her immediately after she was confirmed dead" Gold said crying.
"I'm sorry Gold but you need to to be strong. I'll ensure he is put to death behind bars but I'm going to need your help" Fredrick said as he wiped the tears off her eyelid with his fingers.
"My help?" Gold asked surprised.
"We need evidence which only you can get. Kennedy will be brought here

tomorrow and I need you to talk to him.
He wel aes
which will be recorded but
don't be scared because he will be in chains and there is nothing he can do to harm you" Fredrick assured Gold.
"I will do it" Gold agreed
"I also got news this morning that Joy and Biaisare planning to hurt you".
"Those bitches" Gold growled and she laughed.
"Hey trust me, I'll make their plans fail" Fredrick said and Gold nodded when he said that because the fact that her mom was killed by Kennedy still breaks her heart.
"I r were alive, I would
have introduced her to Fredrick but then she's gone, gone forever but I'll make sure Kennedy pays for all his crimes.
KENNEDY POV
Kennedy sat on the floor in his sitting room frustrated.

"IvI'veost everything all because of that a girl called Gold" Kennedy Lamented bitterly as he gulped down a large the volume of alcohol down his throat.
"I will make you pay Gold" he yelled smashing the bottle on the floor and placing his head in between his knees as he sulked.
He heard the bell chime and he staggered to the door but he opened the door and got the shock of his life.
"What are you two doing here?" Kennedy asked looking at the two men who came to pick Gold up when he sold her.
"It's great you remember us but we are here for you this time"
"What do you mean?" Kennedy asked them.
"I mean its time for you to pay for your sins" One of them answered as he sprayed something on his face and immediately he felt dizzy than he slumped on the floor and blacked out.

JOY POV (Point of View)

"I already got the guys for the job" Bianca said to her

"Are you sure they're professionals?" Joy asked.

"Very sure. We just need to look for a perfect time to strike"

"That's right we need a mole because that Gold girl doesn't go out often"

"Yes you are right" Bianca consented but they were interrupted when they heard the bell ring so they exchanged looks..

"Are you expecting anyone?" Joy asked Bianca

"No but let me go get the door" Bianca said as she rushed to the door and opened it. She and the person spoke for some seconds before she allowed him in.

"Who is he?" Joy asked

"I am Dave and I have something that may interest you" he smirked sitting on the couch.

"What is it?"
"I have been stalking you two for some days and I know you plan on killing Gold he gasped as he said that.
"How..." they asked surprised
"I dislike her as well so I can help you guys in bringing her down" Dave said convincingly
"Why do you want to help us?" Bianca asked..
"It's the least I can do for my sister Avala, she was killed because of that Gold. She framed her and asked Master Fredrick to have her killed" Dave said sobbing.
"So you are one of Fredrick's men?" Joy asked smiling
"Your end is near Gold and you've got too many enemies" Joy muttered inwardly
"Yes I'm Miss Gold's driver actually"
"How are we sure we can trust you?"
"I can't lie to you, I need revenge for my sister" Dave said as he smiled to himself

because he's the mole they've been looking for.
"Good, so tell us what you know" Joy said to him
"I overheard her telling the Master that she would love to go for shopping tomorrow" Dave said.
"Shopping? do you know the boutique she likes to shop in?" Joy asked with a determined look.
"Alexis Boutique. I will notify you when she leaves the house" Dave said to them.
"Perfect Bianca, make contact with the men we are striking with tomorrow" Joy instructed Bianca who nodded and went to communicate with them.
"Here is the plan you will be the one driving her tomorrow then half way to the boutique, I don't care how you do but you must stop the car. Then the boys will come in and kidnap her after which I will like to put a bullet in her head myself" Joy said smiling.
"Let's see how you survive this because

after tomorrow Fredrick will be mine and you will be dead but it's too bad that you won't be alive to watch me take Fredrick from you" Joy said triumphantly to herself.

GOLD POV

"Did they believe you?" Gold asked Dave as she sat on Fredrick's lap resting her head on his shoulders as she watch them talk.

"Yeah, although I never expected that they could be that gullible'"

"So what's their plan?"

"As expected they will take the opportunity to strike tomorrow. I was asked to stop the car half way after which they planned on kidnapping and killing Miss Gold", Dave said.

"Those bitches" Gold groaned.

"Calm down baby, I got this ok" Fredrick said and Gold nodded.

"But what I don't understand is why Joy choose to drag Bianca into it when she

could take care of it herself" Gold asked.
"To implicate Bianca of course incase anything goes wrong because she wouldn't want to suffer alone.
Bianca is the one contacting the assassins that means they know her as their boss and not Joy. She's only using her and at the end she will get rid of her, that's how desperate she is" Fredrick said.
"So bro, what's your plan?" Ethan asked.
"The plan is simple we set a trap for them. Gold won't be the one in the car because someone else who is dressed like her would and hence the car is tinted, they won't get to see the person in it.
They will stop the car exactly where she asks them to but before then, we need to notify the police so they will be waiting to lay ambush on the kidnapers.
I believe they will apprehend them and Janet will be implicated then as for Joy, I know just how to deal with her because she won't escape this" Fredrick said and

Gold looked at him amazed by his way of reasoning.
"Seriously, I think you should be in the police force to join in crime fighting" Gold said and they all chuckled.
"Bro your girlfriend is right, policing is your calling so embrace it with your full chest" Ethan said to Fredrick.
"Bad joke," Fredrick said as he huffed.
"Whatever, see you around bro" Ethan said standing up.
"I want everything to go as planned"
"Yeah sure thing" Fredrick smiled before walking away with Dave.
"Seriously? you really want me to be a police man?" Frederick smirks.
"Not really, I'm not cut out for the stress associated with it like waiting all night for you to come home, having panic attacks when you are going for an operation come on I'm not ready to die young" But Fredrick chuckled.

"Seriously? but you suggested it" Fredrick said.
"That was a joke, I don't want to be a widow at an early age" Gold whispered the last part.
"What did you say?" Frederick said
"Nothing" she smiled nervously.
"Really, I thought I heard you say something" Fredrick said biting his lips and he couldn't help but stare at her but as he leans closer and pulled her into a slow and passionate kiss.
She kissed him back wrapping her arms around his shoulders as he deepened the kiss and their tongues danced in a perfect rhythm and his hands grabbed hold of her butts.
She moaned in his mouth and he slowly pulls out of the kiss and they starred at each other for some seconds trying to catch our breath.
"You will get what you want soon" Fredrick whispered staring at her.

"What?"
"You heard me" Fredrick smirks.
"Could he have possibly heard what I said and does it mean I'm going to be his wife soon?" Gold thought inwardly
Ol48
She sighed dialing her dad's number from her phone book after the discussion she had with Fredrick earlier.
Gold felt she needed to give him a call so she dialed his number and after few rings, he responded
"Hello who is this speaking?" Collins asked and Gold smiled hearing hs voice.
"Dad..." she called.
"Mama is that you? Oh my God I thought I will never hear from you again. Gold I'm really sorry for abandoning you and I Regret it. I thought you would be happy there but I never knew he would do such a monstrous thing to you, Mama, I'm sorry" Collins apologized and Gold felt tears slid down her eyes as he pleaded.

"Dad it's fine, I forgive you already. I'm just glad you are okay. I heard that beast tried to kill you" Gold said.
"He did and I almost lost my life but luckily some guys saved me and they told me everything Gold and that you are also dating their master"
"Oh", Gold said blushing.
"But is that okay with you?" Gold asked nervously.
"'Sure, you are old enough to make decisions for yourself" Collins said
"Thanks ,,dad and Kennedy will be brought to book soon. You can't believe he killed mom" Gold said sadly
"About your mother... " Collins wanted saying but he paused
"What about her? Dad talk to talks Gold said anxiously because she heard him sigh like he wanted to tell her something but he stopped.
"I feel like I caused her death because I wasn't a good husband to her.

If we hadn't divorced, she would still be alive today" Collins said remorsefully.
"Dad it's not your fault. I'm going to make sure her murderer is put to death. Kennedy needs to pay for his sins"
"I know Gold and this time he's going down for good" Collins said and Gold smiled softly wiping the tears off her eyes.
"I love you dad", Gold said as she burst into tears.
"I love you too Mama please take care of yourself" Collins said
"I will dad and take care of you too Bye" Gold said
"Bye" Collins said and Gold smiled cleaning her tears as she ended the call.
"Was that your dad?" Frederick asked walking out of the bathroom with a towel wrapped around his waist.
"Yeah" Gold replied biting her lips and staring at his body. She has seen his body a couple of times but she couldn't help

but drool allover him.
"Are you done checking me out?" Frederick asked and she looked away.
"I wasn't looking" Gold whispered to herself as she felt his presence around her and he smiled. His hands curl around her waist pulling her to himself and he crushed his lips against hers as he slowly got on top of her.

Chapter 6

Gold kissed him back vigorously as their tongues fought for dominance. His hands slide into her shirt as he cups her breast and she moaned softly in his mouth then he felt his fingers rub circles on her nipples.
She gasped softly when she felt his fingers inside her panties.
"Damn FFreddieyou're so irresistible" Gold whispered
"I know He answered smirking as two of his fingers slide into her wet core.
After an intense moment with Gold, Fredrick excused himself from the room to contact Dave hence Gold was asleep and he wouldn't want to disturb her.
"Make sure it goes according to plan" Fredrick said to Dave.
"It will bos,,,s" Dave said smiling as he drove the car out. He drove to the boutique and stopped the car exactly

where he was told to and only few vehicles could be seen along the supposed busy road.

"It seems the police had cleared the area off people to prevent casualties" Dave said but instantly a car sped towards them and almost immediately four armed and masked men came out of the They shot at the car leaving several bullet shots on the car and broken windscreen then the occupants of the car bent their heads down to avoid stray bullets from touching them.

"Get down" The kidnappers yelled as one of them made to open the car door.

"Freeze and drop your weapons down because you ary"

An officer spoke with a megaphone and the policemen began to troop out in their numbery surrounding them.

"Shit, It's a tr,ap," The kidnappers said pointing guns at the policemen but

pulling the trigger would be a death warrant. If they want to stay alive, the only option was to surrender.
"Put down your weapons now" The officer repeated again
"Never" one of them yelled but before he could pull the trigger, he was shot dead in the pool of hwn d.
The other kidnappers watched as their colleague fell to the ground dead and they didn't want to end up like him so they dropped their guns on the floor.
"Shit "one of the kidnappers s,,aid lookin,g at his colleague who was already dead.
"Kick it now" The police ordered and they kicked the guns far from their reach and the captain signaled for three officers to handcuff them and they were forced into the police car.
Soon, an Ambulance came putting the dead body into a body bag and it was transported to the hospital morgue.

BIANCA POV

Bianca was in her home watching TV when her door bell rang. She was worried because she hadn't gotten news from the kidnappers.

"Maybe it's Joy" Bianca thought and went to the do,or. She slide the door open and made to lock slides she sighted the policemen and worst part the kidnappers came with them but before she could lock the door, the policemen forced it open barging into her house.

"She's the one" one of the kidnappers pointed at her and she saw that his face looked badly bruised as they all looked like they were tortured.

"I don't know what you are talking about and do you know In sue you for breaking, knowIng and also invading my privacy"

"Miss Bianca, you are under arrest for

the attempted kidnap of Miss Gold Collins. You have the right to remain silent because whatever you say here will be used against you in the law court" One of the policemen said to her.

"I don't know what you are talking about officer and I do these now this people" she defended.

"Miss Bianca kindly follow us to the station" The officer said.

"Show me your arrest warrant" Bianca said and the policeman handed the paper to her and she read every word on it. She really was under arrest but what about Joy, after all they planned this together.

"Now move" The police officer said to her and she started shedding tears.

"Joy is also involved in this you can't arrest just me" Bianca said angrily

"When you get to the station, you drop your statement" A policeman said as he

handcuffed her.
"I'm innocent, Joy made me do this" Bianca cried as she was dragged forcefully by the policemen.
FREDERICK POV
Fredrick rang the door bell and Joy quickly opened the door getting excited when she saw him.
"Fredrick" She called and went to hug her but he pushed her off him.
"Fredrick, you know I love you please quit treating me this way" Joy said pouting but he didn't say a word to her.
"Please come inside" Joy said holding his hands as she dragged him inside.
"What do I offer you? Red wine, white wine or water?" Joy asked.
"Nothing, I actually came here for something important" Fredrick said observing her sitting room.

"Important, what could that be?" Joy wondered.
"Don't try to play dumb with me. You attempted to kidnap and kill my girlfriend but what did I tell you about not laying a finger on her?" Frederick yelled and she flinched.
"She has used black magic on you Fredrick, she deserves to die and rot in hell" Joy said
"Do you know I can send you to jail for this?" Fredrick said.
"Send mne to jail, then feel free but I will surely come out and kill both of you If You love her so much then die with her" Joy yelled.
"What about a death sentence?" Fredrick asked
"You can't Fredrick, kidnapping doesn't require a death sentence" Joy said as she chuckled.

"What about murder? jut like how you murdered your late husband and brother?" Fredrick said and Joy gasped when he said that.
"How?.. How?..." Joy asked stammering
"How heartless can you be? Imagine killing your own husband. how amature you wouldn't kill me if I make you my girlfriend?"
"I would never do that to you, I did it for you Fredrick" Joy said.
"Did it for me? How could you possibly do it for me?" Frederick asked.
"I never loved him despite the fact that he treated me nicely but I always wanted you so I poisoned him slowly for two years before he died. I did it for the love I had for you" Joy said.
"Then what about your brother? did you also do that for me? Frederick asked
"He called me a slut so I tampered with

his brakes then he had an accident and died"
"You are heartless Joy Imagine killing your husband and brother for some stupid reasons.
I've told you countless times that what we had back then in school was just a fling but you allowed it get into your head" Frederick said sounding angry.
"You will go to jail Joy and you will be put to death for your crimes I'm gonna make sure of it" Fredrick said assuredly.
"You can't do that Fredrick, You can't do that to me" Joy said
"I can Joy" Fredrick smirked showing her his phone that had been recording all she said.
"Fredrick you bastard" Joy yelled
"What, don't you want me again?" Frederick asked smirked in a mocking tune and just then, the police pushed her

door open.
"See you in court Joy and Farewell" Fredrick said winking before leaving the policemen to do their job.
After apprehending Bianca and Joy, a a week later Bianca was set free while Joy still remained in police custody and Joy's cousin Claire went to the station to visit her.
On her arrival Joy began telling her things like trying to play the victim so she'll gain her cousin's sympathy.
"Claire, I need your help on something. you know we are sisters and blood is thicker than water.
"Ok, what do you want me to do for you" Claire asked uninterestedly.
"I want you to help me contact some thugs to help me deal with Fredrick and if possible kill Gold"
"And what do I stand to gain àfter all my

effort hence you're still in jail" Claire asked Joy

"Claire, I make sure you live largely, anything you want just name it and I'll give it to you" Joy said convincingly to Claire.

"I can see that you are insane Joy. So you plan on dragging me down with you just like you almost did to Janet. You are very heartless and you deserve what is coming your way"

"Claire" Joy called surprised because she thought she had gained her attention already but it seems she Is far from it.

"I didn't come here to plan evil with you Joy, I only came to give you this" Claire said and a hot slap landed on Joy's cheeks and she stood up in anger clenching her handcuffed hands in anger

"How dare you, if I weren't in cuffs Claire, I would have given you the the beating of your life" Joy said angrily to

Claire as she
was unable to do anything.
"That's for killing Mike" Claire yelled back and another slap landed on Joy's cheeks. but a warden immediately approached them.
"What is going on here?" The warden questioned
"This demon is planning evil against Fredrick please take her away" Claire said to the warden
"So you are in jail but you are still plotting evil" The warden scolded and pushed Joy forcefully out of the visitors waiting area.
"You will pay for this Claire" Joy said as she glared at her.
"We will see about that" Claire yelled after her
"Bitch" Joy cursed under her breath.

"Shut up and move it you hardened criminal" The warden said.

FREDERICK POV

"Good job, always keep me posted" Fredrick said as he smirked ending the phone call.

He dropped the phone on the light stand and turned to Gold on the bed cuddling her into his arms.

"Freddie, what was that all about?" Gold asked but Fredrick kissed her forehead and stared at her.

"It was the warden I asked to stay close to Joy, just in case she's planning evil and she was planning evil. She tried to talk her cousin into harming me but she refused" Fredrick said to Gold

"That girl doesn't give up" Gold said.

"She shouldn't be your problem baby because she definitely will go down, just sleep" Fredrick said as he stroked Gold's

"Shut up and move it you hardened criminal" The warden said.

FREDERICK POV

"Good job, always keep me posted" Fredrick said as he smirked ending the phone call.

He dropped the phone on the light stand and turned to Gold on the bed cuddling her into his arms.

"Fredie what was that all about?" Gold asked but Fredrick kissed her forehead and stared at her.

"It was the warden I asked to stay close to Joy just in case she's planning evil and actually she was planning evil. She tried to talk her cousin into harming me but she refused" Fredrick said to Gold

"That girl doesn't give up" Gold said.

"She shouldn't be your problem baby because she definitely will go down, just sleep" Fredrick said as he stroked Gold's

body and she nodded with a smile.
"That reminds me, Bianca came over when you were at work" Gold said trailing her fingers on his chest.
"To apologize right? She came to the office as well butI instructed my secretary not to allow her in" Fredrick said emotionlessly.
"Why would you do that baby, that was harsh" Gold said condemning his actions
"Really? If you didn't talk me into setting her free, she would be in jail now but the fact still remains that she tried to kill you and she's really pissing me off"
"But she apologized already so stop being cold hearted" Gold said but Fredrick felt hurt by her words as he flashed back to his parents.
"How could you do that? You are just a cold hearted monIter and i regret marrying you" That was his mum's words to his father.

Frederick hated being called cold hearted but Gold just did and it hurts badly that she just called him cold hearted all because he was looking out for her.
"CoCold-hearted wally" Fredrick said and pushed Gold off and got out of bed.
"Frederick I'm sorry" Gold apologized but Fredrick wasn't hearing any of it.
"Just go to sleep Gold. I need to be left alone" Fredrick told her and walked out of the room.
KENNEDY POV
After Fredrick brought him back to Abuja, he was arrested and sent to jail. He was going to be arraigned in court two days from now. He was in deep thoughts when the sight of someone entering his cell interrupted him.
"What are you doing here?" Kennedy

asked Aeriel because she's one of the reasons why he was in a mess.
"I just came to make sure you don't include me in your deeds" Ariel said.
"My deeds? you told me Irene was cheating on me and you made me kill her"
"'She was cheating with my husband you fool, but I never asked you to rape her useless daughter. You just couldn't keep your dick in your pants" Ariel said mockingly to Kennedy.
"Don't you dare insult me" Kennedy warned but Aerial interrupted.
"What are you going to do, you are locked up here by the person you raped, how hilarious? but what I don't get is how she managed to do that"
"She's fucking a rich dude Fredrick Majesty" Kennedy said and Ariel gasped.

Frederick Majesty?" Aerial asked in surprise
"Do you know him?" Kennedy asked.
"Of course, he's one of the richest men in Lagos but what the hell did he see in that girl?"
"That's not my business I need to leave this place Asap" Kennedy said.
"You can't my dear he is damn too rich and there is no hope for you. Just be a good boy and don't talk" she smiled and stood up to leave.
"I guess he's coming to Abuja then, I should go get my daughter ready to steal him away from her.
"She doesn't deserve someone that good" Aerial smiled and walked away.
GOLD POV
"Why would you say that to him?" Ella

scolded when Gold narrated whàt transpired between herself and Fredrick the previous night.

"It was stupid of me to have said that I know but the worst part of it was that he didn't sleep in the room and early this morning, he went to work so I didn't get the chance to apologize properly.

I'm just so confused and angry at myself but I don't want to loose Fredrick because I love him" Gold said crying.

"You are not loosing him Gold and if there is one thing thing I, it's that he loves you so much" Ella assured Gold who was crying uncontrollably.

"I know that but he has never behaved this way before and it feels like I hurt him so bad" Gold said

"Worry no more Gold, he will surely come around. The way to a man's heart is through his stomach" Ella said giggling.

"Yes Ella, I should cook for him his

favorite food and go to his office" Gold said
"Exactly, he will surely forgive you after that and you guys might end up making love in the office" Ella said grinning and Gold blushed slightly.
"You are crazy" Gold said laughing uncontrollably
"We both know, I'm saying the truth" Ella said laughing out loud.

FLOURISH POV
Flourish smiled to herself with a cup of coffee in her hands waiting for him to walk up to her then she sighed when she sighted him.
Here we go" She muttered and as he proceeded to walk past her she pretended to bump into him pouring the coffee on his shirt.
"Oh Dave I'm so sorry"

Chapter 7

"What the hell Flourish? Can't you look where you are going to" Dave asked angrily
"Im sorry but let me help you clean it up " Flourish volunteered.
"Never mind" He angrily dropped the food basket on his table and hurried to the bathroom.
She smiled looking around to be sure no one was looking then she carried the food basket, opened the food flask and sprinkled some substance into it before closing the food flask and adjusting the food basket.
She sat on her table and waiting for him to come back but he walks to her table and picked up his food basket.
"Clumsy secretary, this shouldn't repeat itself again" Dave said.
"It won't" Flourish said smirking as she watched him walk into the boss's office.
"Things are about to fall into place and

he's so going to fall into my arms now" Flourish said happily.

"Hi Bianca right?" Gold said

"Oh yes Miss Gold it's so nice to have you here again" Bianca said smiling.

"Thanks but is my boyfriend in the office " Gold asked

"He is really busy now but hence you are his girlfriend, he would want to see you" Bianca responded

"OK ,,thanks" Gold said smiling as she walked to the elevator with Chike following closely behind with the food basket in his hands.

She pressed a button on the elevator and the door slide opened and they went in as it immediately closes.

She went towards the direction of Fredrick's office but stopped when she sighted a girl adjusting her skirt and shirt but she looked disturbed so she really didn't notice Gold's presence.

"That man is really a cold stone, I can't believe after adding the sex pill to his food, he still refused to fuck me and the worst part is that he even fired me.
"He is really horny right now, so I can try again but this time, I'm going strip in front of him and he definitely won't resist me" she mutters to herself.
So this bitch actually tried to seduce my man.
"Uhmm Uhmm" Gold pretended to cough and the lady turned to look at her with a shocked expression.
Gold gave Chike a 'teach her a lesson' look and he nodded slightly then she took the food basket from him and glared at her before walking into his office.
She shut the door behind her locking it properly and stared at Fredrick as he paced round the office.
He was too deep in thoughts to notice her presence. and to think that he actually had the chance to cheat on her despite

being drugged but he refused and it made her love him even more.
"Frederick" Gold called then he turned to see her standing by the door. Knowing he was horny she decided to tease him a little.
"Baby don't tell me you are still mad at me" Gold said as she dropped the food basket on the table. But Fredrick walked up to her, kissed her roughly and he carried her on his torso.
"Darling are you Ok?" Gold asked in between kisses pretending she had no the idea about what happened.
"I will be alright after I fuck you" Fredrick whispered to her as he cleared off his office table and kept her on it.
He kissed her again as he took off his suit jacket and quickly unbuttoned his tie and his hands slid up her hip, raised her dress up to her waist.
He broke the kiss and unbuckled his belt staring intensely at her before unzipping his zipper then brought out his very

hard dick.
"Damn, baby you are so hard"
"Some bitch added a sex pill to my food" he whispers into her ears as he shifted her panties aside.
"You should probably see a doctor" Gold whispered in a sultry voice as he guides his length to her entrance.
"Then be my doctor" Fredrick said as he slowly penetrates her already wet core and they both moaned at the penetration then he began to thrust slowly into her as he quickly picked up a fast pace.
"Damn this feels so good" Fredrick moaned kissing her tenderly while she dug her fingers into his back, loving the feeling of having him inside of her.
Gold moaned loudly aching her head backwards as Fredrick continued digging into her wet core. He groaned as he assisted her take off her dress completely.
He smirked when he saw that she wasn't putting on a bra so he took one of her

nipples in his mouth and he banged her hard on the table.
"Baby ahhhhh" Gold moaned flexing her hips forward to meet his thrust as he made her lie flat on the table thern she hanged her legs on his shoulders holding unto the table for support.
Gold moaned loudly as her orgasm reached it's peak and Fredrick groaned loudly as he pounded away into her dripping core, crashing his lips against hers as her body quaked violently and her orgasm broke then she gasped out loudly as he lifted her up from table.
He took hold of her ass with his hands as he thrust into her with full speed then he kissed her and she reciprocated aggressively with her back touching the wall.
Their loud moans, raged breathing and the slurping sound of her core produced as he pounded her against the wall filled the entire room and she moaned loudly against his lips and they climaxed again.

"I want you to ride me baby" Fredrick whispered into her ears and she gasp slightly and he carried her from the wall and sat with her on his office chair making her straddle him.

Gold kissed him as she helped him unbutton and took off his dress which was all sweaty. He moaned as he guided his length back into her moaning softly as Gold rocked her core on his erection then he grabbed hold of her ass and took one of her nipples in his lips and tease the other nipple with his finger.

"Keep going baby," Fredrick said as Gold moaned then he slammed her core harder with his length then she moaned as her body quaked violently and she came again.

He bent her against the table then he penetrated her, thrusting in with so much vigor while she moaned in pleasure as he kissed her from behind spanking her ass softly.

"Oh my God shit I'm gonna cum"

Fredrick groaned loudly as he pounded her dripping core then her body quake violently as her core tightened around his length and they both came.
Frederick turned her around as he crushed his lips against hers and Gold reciprocated slowly but then he slowly disengaged from the kiss and smiled.
"I love you Gold" Frederick said passionately to Gold.
"I love you too Fredrick but I'm definitely going to need a massage because you almost broke my waist" Gold said but Fredrick chuckled softly.
"It's not funny," Gold said as she frowned.
"We are both getting that massage when we get home"
"Also, you need to see a doctor because drugs like this could have some side effects" Gold said
"You are right baby but you are coming with me" Fredrick said
"Thanks baby for not cheating on me" Gold said to Fredrick and he smiled.

"I woulcheatver chea,t on you my love, you mean the world to me"
"Same here Sweetheart and I'm sorry about yesterday" Gold said apologetically
"It's fine Gold come on let's go freshen up in the bathroom" Fredrick said as he giggled and lifted Gold up carrying her on his arms in a bridal style to the bathroom.
After bathing they both wore clothes but the room smelt of sex, so he sprayed an air freshener in the room, sat on his office chair and Gold smiled sitting on his laps.
"I want to eat what you brought" Fredrick said as he smirked at Gold
"Sure" she replied and brought out the food from the basket setting it on the table then he smiled as he perceived the the aroma of the food.
"My God, it's my favorite Fredrick said. I never knew you could cook sea foods" he said as he raised his brows at Gold.
"I did not actually, Ella prepared it while

I watched her do it. Just a little more practice and I would become a master in it" Gold boasted and he smiled.

"I know you would"

"Come on eat up," Gold said then he picked his chopsticks and started eating.

"It's nice, come on have some" Frederick said as he fed her with the food. Soon when they finished eating the food together, Gold cleared out the dishes and put them in the food basket while Frederick picks up his telephone and placed the receiver on his ears dialing a number on it.

"See me in my office now" he said and ended the call and Few minutes later, they heard a knock on the door.

"Come in" Fredrick said and Dave walked into the office

"You sent for me boss"

"What's the meaning of this nonsense?" he asked referring to the food that he had brought earlier but Dave was confused as he seem not to understand

"I don't understand" Dave said.
"How the hell did you allow Flourish put a sex pill into my food"
"What, a sex pill? She had earlier poured coffee on me soI had to drop the food on her table to use the bathroom. I'm very sorry about that please" David pleaded.
"Sorry, What if I was poisoned? How would you leave my food on her table?" Frederick asked angrily.
"Baby please take it easy" Gold sighs and he tried to keep his calm.
"I'm really sorry sir, It would never happen again" Dave assured
"It better not. Take the food away and leave" Fredrick instructed
"One more thing boss, we have a new secretary already and he met up all the requirements" Dave announced
"Tell the human resource manager to bring him into my office"

",OK bos,s" Dave said taking the food away and left.
"You are hiring a male secretary?" Gold asked surprised
"Yeah, the female ones all gave me headaches but come to think of it, having a male secretary, he might end up flirting with you..." Frederick said jealousy.
"Don't tell me you are jealous?" Gold asked grinning.
"You are my girlfriend and I have the right to be jealous" he pouted and she laughed.
"You look so cute when you are jealous" Gold says.
"Are you seriously flirting with me?" Fredrick asked as he rolled his eyes at her.
"You're my boyfriend right" Gold said and he chuckled and pulled her into a kiss but it was interrupted by someone who knocked on the door so he reluctantly pulled out of the kiss.

"Come in" Gold said as she rested her head on Fredrick's chest then twO men stepped in.
Onemiddle-aged aged man who should be In his late thirties which Gold assumed was the hiring manager and the other was young guy was twho he new secretary.
"Good day Sir" they both greeted.
"Good day Miss Gold" the hiring manager said smiling at her and she smiled back.
"Seat" Frederick said to them and they both sat on the chairs opposite him.
"Sir this is Mr Goliath, your new secretary"
"Nice to meet, you Sir" Goliath said and smiled at Fredrick and also stole glances at Gold.
"I don't havc much to say just do your work diligently and you won't get fired" Fredrick said but Goliath kept stealing glances at Gold and she became uncomfortable.

"What's up with him?" Gold thought but Fredrick already noticed the way he constantly glared at Gold and he had an angry look on hs face.
"Thank you sir" Goliath said but Fredrick interrupted him.
"One more thing, you see this lady right here, she's totally off limits. She's mine and if you don't want to get fired on your first day you stay clear" fRederick said and Goliath became scared.
"Yes sir and I'm sorry" Goliath replied feeling uneasy and Gold chuckled silently.
FREDERICK POV
"The guts of this man staring at my woman that way in front of me" Fredrick thought inwardly
"Mr Fidelis, brief him of his duties so he can commence work properly tomorrow. That would be all you both can leave" Fredrick said to them.
"Yes Sir" they both stood up and left shutting the door properly.

"Can you imagine the nerve of him to stare at you like that?" Frederick huffed angrily and she smiled.
"Don't tell me you are jealous?"
"I have every right to be because you are mine baby"
"You said it yourself My love, I'm all yours so your secretary should be the least of your worries.
No one can compete with you because of me. it's you I want Fredie, just you" Gold said and Fredrick let out a smile when she said that.
"It feels so good hearing you say that Gold but from the look of things that guy is going to get fired in less than three days" Fredrick said and Gold chuckled.
"Seriously?" She said laughing out loud.
"Yeah, you should be my secretary instead" Fredrick said as he winked.
"What? no way, I didn't even go to the university" Gold said.

"Do you still want to go to school?" Frederick asked and He nodded.
"Yeah and I want to major in SLT"
"SLT? So you are a science major after all
"Yeah"
"You already took JAMB right?"
"Yes I have"
"what was your JAMB score?" Frederick asked
"250" Gold replied and Fredrick's jaw dropped as she said that.
"You got to be kidding me baby" He said amazed but she chuckled.
"Well I'm not" Gold responded laughing
"That score is awesome, you almost had a complete 300"
"I know, my mum freaked out too and so did I. I had initially set my hopes on 159 but I got the shock of my life when I saw the score and I was like is this score mine

?" Gold said happily.
"Well sometimes, we usually then more then what we expected and sometimes less" Fredrick responded
"Yeah, true"
"]ust get all your necessary documents, Il process your admission into the National Open University at Abuja"
"What? That's the best university in Abuja and I heard it's very hard to get in" she pouted and chuckled.
"You seem to be forgetting who you are dating"
"How can I forget that? Frederick Majesty, one of the most famous, cutest and the richest man in Africa is my boyfriend" Gold giggled and simmered mgl glad didn't forget. You will begin the stool once you're ready ok?" Frederick said
"Yeah sure" Gold responded
"How are you going to cope with being my wife and going to college?" Frederick

muttered inaudibly.
"Huh, what did you say?" Gold asked smiling.
"Never mind," Fredrick said as he chuckled softly.

Chapter 8

"You aren't going to talk are you?" Gold asked trailing her fingers on his chest.
"Kiss me first" Fredrick bite his lips as he stared at her.
"That won't be a problem" Gold answered and wrapped her arms around his neck staring at his face and then his lips.
The grip he had on her waist tightened and she gasped slightly then she leans closer and slowly claimed his lips in hers
His eyes flutter shut as she kissed him back letting her take control and their tongues danced rhythmically as their breathing increased.
Fredrick's fingers went down her cheeks slowly as she kissed him more aggressively pushing her tongue further into his mouth then he bits her bottom lip softly as she pulled out the kiss ancurledmirk curled on his face.

"Not bad, but I still won't tell you" Fredrick said but Gold frowned at him.
"Frederick, you are so scheming and a tease" Gold said as she huffed silently.
"That's because you look so cute when I tease you" Fredrick said making a funny the face that made her laugh.
"That's how you look when you are being teased"
"That's not how I look?" she protested and he chuckled then she rested her head on his chest sighing softly.
"Frederick, did you go to college?"
"No baby I didn't"
"Seriously but Why?" Gold asked
"That's going to lead to a very long story" Frederick responded
"Well, I want to hear it"...
"Well because that was when dad and mom died and I had to take over the Company at the age of nineteen.

At that time, my uncle kicked against it, he was always so greedy and he wanted to take the company for himself.
He has always been in rivalry with my dad and I just couldn't watch him take Hawass ours"
"So did he let you take over easily?"
"No, he didn't, he convinced the board members that I was just a secondary school graduate with no college certificate and they revolted so I decided to strike a deal with them"
"A deal how?"
"As at then, the company was facing a lot of crises and I was made to temporarily take over for five months to resolve those crises. And that was when I showed them my business skills.
I knew I was going to be the CEO someday and I had prepared myself for it since I was a kid and I had two great teachers, my dad and myself. Later I enrolled in an online business class too. I didn't just solve those crises

but I also made a remarkable change in the company and that alone made me earn respect from the board members and I succeeded in beating my uncle to the game"

"Wow you are such a genius but what did your uncle then do?"

"He got angry, withdrew his shares and started his own company. He also tried to get some of my investors but they all had faith in me and didn't withdraw their funds.

He decided to manufacture electronic products like ours making us business rival but I knew he would do something like that so I had two backup plans"

"What were the plans?" Gold asked.

"Introducing a new line of products that will shake the market and also making the company is a dual production company

"What was the other product?"

"Agricultural products" I grinned.

"You wanted to kill your uncle with your wisdom" Gold said and Fredrick chuckled at her words.
"He asked for it," Frederick said as he rolled his eyes.
"So which of the factories do the male servants at home work in?"
"The agricultural factory and it's located far away from the company building" Fredrick said.
"Is your uncle still your rival?"
"Not anymore, he retired and now his son Austin Damon is in charge.
He's my very annoying cousin and just like his father, he wants to obtain what I have" Fredrick said.
"You sound like you hate him a lot" Gold asked.
"I do and I bet you will hate him too" Fredrick assured
"If you don't like him, then I don't like him too" Gold said and Fredrick

smiled.
"That's more like it," He said kissing her passionately.

GOLIATH POV
Goliath sigh tiredly from the boring lecture Mr. Fidelis was giving because that wasn't what he was looking for.
"Are we done?" Goliath asked Mr. Fidelis
"You are so not ready for work" Mr Fidelis said
your boss is always that way, Bossy and cold? Goliath asked.
"He's the boss so he has to be bossy but what were you expecting? You were the one at fault because you
just couldn't get my eyes off his woman
" Mr. Fidelis said defensively.
"She's pretty and you really can't blame me you know?" Goliath said smiling.
"Well those eyes of yours will definitely get you into trouble"

"I think she is unlucky to have a cold guy as a boyfriend"
"Are you crazy? Any girl would kill to be in her position" Mr. Fidelis fired back.
"Whatever, it's obvious that she's after his money. No woman would want to stay with him" Goliath replied confidently.
"Miss Gold looks like a responsible lady and they are both happy together so you should mind your business mister and for your information, he has fired two of his secretaries because of that lady.
If you don't want to be the third, stay clear" Mr. Fidelis warned Goliath.
"Who would want to miss this opportunity? This company is a really big one and I bet you guys have wonderful ideas just look at how big the company is. Do you mind sharing some ideas with me?" Goliath asked grinning hoping Mr. Fidelis would take the bait.
"Sure but that would be tomorrow. You can leave now and make sure you report

early to work tomorrow.w" Mr. Fidelis said.
"Ok sir" Goliath replied and walked out of his office.
"Never knew it would be this easy to get the info from this Gullible old man" Goliath thought.
"But Gold is a beautiful lady and taking her from him won't be a bad idea at all so Mr. Frederick Sir, your end is near" Goliath said inwardly before releasing a dangerous smile.
<br data-mce-bogus="1">
GOLD. POV
"He asked that?" Frederick asked Mr. Fidelis
"Yeah sir and just as you said before the interview, he asked about ideas the boss has" Mr. Fidelis said.
"I was right, after all, he's Austin's that fool doesn't give up. Good job Fidelis and for this, you will get a twenty percent increase in your salary" Fredrick said and Mr. Fidelis reacted happily.

"Thank you sir" Mr. Fidelis appreciated Fredrick gratefully.
"It's nothing, you can leave now" Fredrick said and Mr. Fidelis smiled and opened the door to leave but he stopped when he saw a guy walk into the room.
"Speak of the devil" Fredrick muttered and two security men came running into
"Sir we are sorry we tried to stop him" but he refused
"Just go, all of you," Fredrick said to them
"Yes sir" the security men replied and left and the unexpected visitor surfaced.
"Is this how you welcome your cousin who just returned from a vacation?" he withheld in a smirk as he sat on the chair opposite them and he looks really annoying.
"What do you want Austin?" Frederick asked.
"Wow I see you found yourself an American beauty" Austin said and rolled

his eyes.
"You should take your eyes off her, you just might go blind" Fredrick warned as he chuckled silently.
"May I know the name of this beauty?" he smirked seriously "This guy doesn't have shame" Gold muttered inwardly.
"You should ask google," Fredrick said to Austin let out a scoff.
"Since you decided not to tell me your name. I would love to invite you to a party" Austin said and he could already feel Fredrick's anger boiling that it would explode any second.
"I'm, not coming," Gold said
"You heard her, Austin so you can leave" M.r Fidelis said
"You really shouldn't let him control you" Austin said referring to Gold.
"Listen to me Austin, Frederick doesn't control me so you should mind your business"

"Playing hard to get right... What Austin wants he gets" Austin said nonchalantly.
"Austin get the fuck out of my office this minute" Fredrick commanded.
"Frederick you really shouldn't let this dumb ass punk anger you. No one can compete with you for me.
Mr. Austin if you don't have anything reasonable to say you should leave now"
"You heard her, get out before I call security on you" Fredrick fired back and he chuckled.
"I will leave but be rest assured that I'll be back" Austin assured them.
ETHAN POV
Immediately after Austin left, Ethan stormed angrily into Fredrick's office
"Bro, what the hell was that bastard doing here?" Ethan asked walking into the office with an angry expression.

"What else if not to look for trouble? Can you Imagine that idiot was practically trying to woo Gold right in front of me"
"Baby, you really shouldn't mind him because there is no way I'll choose him over you. He's annoying but you are sweet and I love you Darling that's all that matters"
"Gold I know you would never do such a thing but Austin is a complete maniac. He was the reason Joy and I broke up even though liked
her though but It's high time, I put him in his place"
"I support you, bro, Austin needs to be thought a lesson"
"Damn it my headaches" Fredrick groaned holding his head.
"Bro are you Ok?" Ethan asked w, worried
"No, I get this headache plus my vision is getting blurred" Fredrick said
"It must be the side effect of the drug, we should take you to a hospital" Gold
with a drip needle inserted into his arms.

"Seriously? baby I'm not dying" Fredrick said.
"I know only that you got me worried" Gold pouted holding his hands.
"I'm fine now baby so worry less" Fredrick smiled with his palm on her cheeks.
"Do you feel much better now?" Ethan asked.
"Yeah" Fredrick responded with a smile.
AUSTIN POV
"That bastard. Why does he always get so lucky?"
"Lee, what is it this time?" His father Mr. Damon asked.
"Nothing much, just that Fredrick found a new girlfriend and I want her"
"If you want her then have her" His dad encouraged.
"It's not so easy because Fredrick has

feed her with lies already."
"What makes you think she wants to be with him? Frederick is just a cold
the monster who doesn't deserve good things
but If you want this girl so much, then have her, after all,l, you're more handsome then he is"
I smiled. "Thanks, dad"
Just then, Goliath walked into the sitting room.
"Good day boss" He greeted Mr. Damon
"How was it?" Mr. Damon asked.
"Great, Fredrick didn't notice, and by tomorrow I get enough information to bring him down" Goliath said
"Great job," Mr. Damon said
"Thanks but Mr... Fredrick has this pretty a girl as his girlfriend s over
protective of her" Goliath said.
"I know that" Austin interrupted
"Well I wa, not he, r," Goliath said

"You can't have her" Austin replied angrily
"And why is that?"
"Because I want her too and as your boss you should step down for me" Austin told him tapping his shoulders.
"But....." Goliath was about to say but Austin interrupted him
"You can go home now sO see yourself through the door"
AERIAL POV
"Mum what is it?" Queen answered her mother impatiently when she called
"Baby I have something important to tell you and you must not speak of this to your father"
"Ok. What is it?"
"It's about your evil step sister"
"Gold, what about her mom? Dad said she would be coming to the states with

her boyfriend and wonder which guy is dumb enough to have her ugly ass as a girlfriend" Queen reply I'm noted not just any guy baby, he's Fredrick Majesty" Aerial replied and Queen gasped.

"How did she get that lucky? Gold doesn't deserve someone that rich someone will try to show up.

Wow so she has a wealthy boyfriend while I'm stuck with this dumb ass RobbinIt'ssIt'sss not for long Queen or don't you want to have a rich boyfriend?"

Of course" Queen Of to be Fredrick's girlfriend?" Her mum answered

"Yeah but mum, Gold would never allow it", Queen said worriedly.

"Forget about that bitch, he's a man so use your charms. After all, your beauty can't be compared withholds"

is impossible"
"I didn't pay you to give me bad news" Joy yelled at him and the lawyer fired back.
"And I didn't tell you to commit huge crimes, if only you had pleaded guilty on the arraignment hearing, you could have been given a life imprisonment verdict. Maybe years later, we could have filed for an appeal but you just don't listen" The Lawyer blasted Joy who literally went mute.
"Is there any way you can help me?" Joy asked politely.
"I'm afraid no, the only way out was rendered useless by you" The lawyer answered.
"I can't die here, I detest you Gold" Joy cried as she lamented.
"You brought this upon yourself" The the lawyer said and walked out on her.

Chapter 9

GOLD POV

She opened the door to their room and smiled as Fredrick just got discharged from the hospital so she decided to give him a sensual massage.

She had to leave the hospital earlier to come set up the room. When Frederick entered the room, he couldn't help but SCream in amazement at how the room was transformed.

"Oh my God" his jaw dropped as he stared at the sight of the room, beautiful candlelight lit up the room making it look very romantic and the bed was decorated with beautiful rose petals.

"Wow Baby this is amazing" Fredrick said smiling

"I'm glad you like it, you should probably change into a towel maybe cause I'm giving you a sensual massage" Gold said biting her lips.

"I'd like that" Fredrick said and they both set out to work.
Gold smiled when she saw Fredrick lie on his stomach with a towel wrapped around his waist. He was already on a simple spa robe while she applied the massage oil to his palm and worked her fingertips slowly on his bare back.
She traced slow, circular patterns up and down the sides of his spine and she heard him gasp.
"Where the hell did you learn how to do that?" Frederick asked.
"Movies I guess,l told him as moved from his spine muscles to the shoulders and then in between his shoulder blades then up to his neck.
"Geez this is way too good to learn movies, s," Fredrick said as he
groaned silently and Gold chuckled.
"What? are you Getting hard already?" Gold asked grinning.

"Maybe" Fredrick replied
"Geez, you are such a pervert," Gold said spanking him slightly on his ass
"Your pervert" He responded and they both burst out laughing.
Golsigheded trailing her fingers slowly on Fredrick's oily chest then after the massage, Fredrick offered to also give her a massage, a hot one at that, and they ended up having sex.
"You know tomorrow is Joy's trial right?"

- "Yeah, I know that"o)

"Get some you will need it"
Fredrick said and slowly Gold closed her eyes.
"Good night Baby" he pecked her forehead.
"Good night"Gold whispered.
The next morning...
Gold smiled nervously as she was ked

hand in hand with Fredrick to the entrance of the courtroom en she smiled faintly at the female lawyer whom Fredrick hired outside the court room.

"Hi I'm Barrister Ola and you must be Gold" she smiled broadly stretching her hands out for a handshake which Gold gladly received.

"Yes I am and I heard you are one of the best" Gold complimented.

"Yes" Barrister Ola nodded slightly still smiling then Gold instantly took a liking to her especially with the way she smiles.

"I see I was completely forgotten" Fredrick shrugged frowning.

"No you weren't" Gold nudged his shoulders slightly and he smiled.

"So Barrister Ola, have you done what I asked you to do?" Fredrick asked.

"Of course and we Frederick"

"Do what Freddie?" Gold asked

"You'll see" Frederick sad as he smirked but he was interrupted by an unwanted

guest.
"Wow wow wow, look who we got here" Austin said smiling as he walked up to them.
What the hell is he doing here?" Gold asked the already upset Fredrick but he ignored her question.
"What do you want Austin?" Fredrick asked calmly
"Your girlfriend Gold" Austin replied fearlessly which made Gold wonder how he got to know her name.
"And oh I did as you said, I asked to google and your name happened to be there. But I happened to find out about your past Gold and it was interesting?" Austin said confidently and Gold huffed silently

but then she looked at her angry boyfriend but his fist were clenched like he was ready to beat this foolish thing up "Baby it's enough" Gold whispered holding his hands.
"Gold you heard what he said"
"Let's just go in, he's not worth our time besides, we are in court" Gold encouraged him and he agreed grudgingly and followed her into the courtroom"I will have you Gold just watch out"
They heard Austin's voice.
"You guys should probably get a restraining order on him" Gold said to Fredrick.
"Like he would obey anyways" Fredrick said as they settled down in a seat in the the court then the proceedings began.
"The prosecutor may noW call out it's

first, witnessnessorge said.
"Thank you, your honor... I'd like to call on my first witness Miss Gold Collins"
Immediately Gold was called Fredrick squeezed her hands softly giving her the go ahead signal then she sighed of relief and walked to the witness box.
"Step in the box please"
"Take an oath of truth before this honorable court"
"I Gold Collins do solemnly, sincerely and truly declare and affirm that the the evidence I shall give shall be the truth the whole truth and nothing but the truth so help me God" Gold declared.
"How well do you know the defendant?" Her lawyer asked.
"I don't know her too well" Gold answered her truthfully.
"In your opinion, what do you think prompted the defendant to kidnap you?

" The lawyer asked again
"Hatred and Jealousy because I got Fredrick and she didn't" Gold said then turned at to look the stand at the end and saw her
let out a scoff.
"Did she in any way threaten you?"
"She didn't need to, it was all over her face"
"That would be all, you may return to your seat"
After Gold was called upon, she later called Fredrick, Bianca, and also the kidnappers. The kidnappers had separate trial dates as they had been involved in many malicious crimes and also because Fredrick didn't file a law it against them but the state.
"Your honor I'd like to call on the defendant"
"You may proceed".
"Miss Joy Martins can you please step

forward" The lawyer said and Joy walked to the witness box and took the court oath.
"Why did you kill your husband Mr. PPhil?"
"I didn't kill him", Joy said...
"You didn't? Do you realize lying to the court while under oath is a serious offense" The lawyer said.
"Really? well I didn't lie about anything" Joy said nonchalantly
"What prompted you to cut the brakes of your brother's car that lead to his death? " The lawyer asked again.
"I don't know what you are talking about"Your honor I want to show the defendant item 1 marked for identification" The lawyer said and the picture was distributed to the judge and was also placed in front of Joy.

She had a surprised look on her face but was quick to hide it. The picture was shown on a large screen for the entire court to see and it was a young teenage girl about her age.

"Do you know the lady in the picture?" The lawyer asked

"I don't" Joy denied

"How do you claim not to know the little the maid who worked for you and your husband? whom you thought you had killed the night you murdered your husband".

"I don't know what you're talking about"

"Your honor I want to cathe ll outa witness

"Proceed," The Judge said then Joy was asked to step down and she headed back to her seat.

"Miss Alice Please step forward for the court to see you" the lawyer said and the

the girl stood up showing the court ."I guess she was the person Fredrick talked about with his lawyer earlier. So he did have this all planned out" Gold thought Inwardly but Joy had a shocked expression as Alice walked to the witness box then she took the oath and step into the witness box.

"Miss Alice can you please tell us your relationship with the defendant" The lawyer asked.

"I was a maid that her husband took pity on and picked me out of the streets to live with them"

"Can you please tell this honorable the court in full detail how she killed her husband and how she tried to kill you?"

"Mrs. Joy would always poison my boss's food at night. I tried to tell him about it but he never believed who would believe a twelve-year-old girl anyways? But whenever she poisoned his food, I would usually switch the food out but

after a year and her husband refused to die, she decided to kill him herself.
That night, I was in my room preparing for my singing audition which was meant to be the following day, suddenly I held muffled screams and without thinking, I sprang out of my bed and headed to their room.
The door was left slightly ajar and I watched her suffocate my boss with a pillow. He struggled with her but then she shot him in the head through the pillow.
I wanted to run but she sighted me and dragged my fearful frame into the room and shot me twice" Alice narrated and she broke into tears and Gold felt like crying as well.
"How could Joy be this wicked?" Gold said out loud
"You may step out of the box please" The the lawyer said then Alice cleaned her eyes and walked back to where she sat.

"Your honor I'd like to call back the defendant" The lawyer requested and the judge approved

"The defendant may now step forward" The lawyer said and Joy walked to the witness box.

"Mrs. Joy, can you please tell the court why you tried to kill an innocent twelve-year-old child?" The lawyer asked Joy in

an angry tone.

"I don't know her, she's just making up lies" Joy screamed in frustration.

"Your honor I'd like to tender this audio recording as exhibit A" the bailiff took the audio from her and played it for the entire court to hear.

"Die Philp, die" They all heard Joy's voice and followed by muffled screams a the gunshot was heard and the scream stopped then Alice's cries were heard as Joy dragged her back.

"Please don't kill me Ma, I promise not to

tell anyone" Alice pleaded
"Too late for that Alice. I always wondered why Philip refused to die after poisoning him for months but now I realized you were the one who swapped out the food each time.
You know too much Alice and the only the way I can be sure that won't talk is for you to die"
"Please don't kill me, please Ma I won't tell anyone to please" Alice cried but Joy wasn't having any of it.
"I'm sorry Alice but In your next life, you will learn to mind your business" Joy said as two sounds of gunshots followed after which the recording stopped.
"So Mrs. Joy can you now please explain to the court what we heard just now?" The lawyer said
"I don't know".
"Mrs. Joy you seem to be forgetting that

you confessed to your crimes
on tape"
"I don't know what you're talking about".
"Your honor I'd like to tender this audio recording as exhibit B" The lawyer said and the recording of how Fredrick made her confession was played for the court to hear.
"Thank you your honor that completes my cross-examination" the lawyer said sitting down.
"The Defense, do you have any cross examinations?" the Judge asked
"No your honor I'd like to give
my closing statement" Joy's lawyer said
"You may proceed" The Judge approved.
"My client Mrs. Joy, committed a lot of crimes even to the extent of trying to kill an innocent child. I'm a lawyer your honor and I cannot turn a blind eye to all she has done. I ask that the jury pass

out its verdict however, it dims fit"
"This is crazy even her lawyer testified against her" Fredrick chuckled
"What, How could you say that? what am I pay you for?" Joy yelled.
"Mrs. Joy, do you realize you are in a courtroom?" The lawyer asked then Joy sighed grudgingly and kept mute.
"The prosecutor may noW give it's the closing statement".
"Your honor the evidence against Mrs Joy is overwhelming even her lawyer testified against her. She is a dangerous criminal that would be toxic to the society if set free.
I ask that the jury would give those people she killed and tried to kill justice and that you may pass out a fair verdict. That would be all your honor" The lawyer said.
"Is the jury's verdict ready?" The judge

asked
"Yes your honor" the jury spokesperson gave the verdict to the judge.
"May the defense and the defendant rise " The Judge requested and both Joy and her lawyer stood up.
"So members of the jury have reached verdict?"The Judge asked then the jury spokesperson stood up and replied.
"Yes, your honor we have."
"Members of the Jury on the Case of Mr Fredrick Majesty vs. Mrs. Joy Martins what do you say?"
"Your Honor, the members of this Jury find the defendant guilty"
"Members of the Jury, this Court dismisses you and thanks you for a job well done" the judge said as he dismissed the jury.
"After much deliberation from the jury, this court finds Miss Joy Martins guilty

beyond reasonable doubt and is hereby sentenced to death by hanging" The the judge declared and Joy was paraded outside but when she saw Fredrick she paused.
"Happy now?" Joy asked in handcuffs while Fredrick wrapped his hands around Gold's waist pulling her to himself.
"Well, I'm happy and sad. I'm happy that you won't be a bother to us and sad that you are leaving. You did a lot of mean things Joy but it still doesn't change the fact that you were my ex.
In your next life be a better person" Fredrick told her as she sheds tears.
"I'm sorry Fredrick for all I did but I don't want to die" Joy pleaded in tears.
"But you have killed people who were close to you. don't you think those people deserved a second chance? It's called justice baby girl and you can't escape it. Officer please take her away" Fredrick

called the attention of the officers.
"Fredrick please" Joy cried as the policemen took her away.
"Wow so touching," Austin said walking into the conversation. "Seriously? doesn't he get tired?"
Gold asked Fredrick silently"
"I'm seriously not in the mood for your nonsense" Fredrick said to him
"I want to talk to Gold alone".
"That's not possible Austin. Go get your own girlfriend and stop running after mine"
"That should be my business and not yours but I still want to talk to Gold"
"Well I don't want to talk to you so stop being a jerk. baby let's just go" Gold said to Fredrick then he smiled broadly as they walked away from Austin.
"You can't run away from me Gold. Houston always got what it wanted, screw your self gold yelled back angrily.

Chapter 10

"Barrister Ola get ready for our next case and it's going to be against Austin" Fredrick said angrily but she chuckled.
"Very funny" Barrister Ola replied.
"Well I'm serious" Fredrick responded
"OK, I should be on my way now" Barrister Ola said and waved at Gold slightly before leaving.
"Are you guys like friends now?" Fredrick asked
"Maybe, but you seem to know her a lot"
"Not really but she happened to be my senior in high school"
"So I guess I should start getting ready to go back to the Abuja" Gold said giggling as they proceeded to the parking lot.
"Yeah and we are leaving tomorrow"
"I can't wait to finally see Esther, I've missed her so much"
"Esther, Ella's twin," Fredrick asked

"Yeah but Fredrick can Ella come with us ? Please" Gold pleaded.
"She can come along if she wants to but she'll have to come back"
"Of course, thanks love" Gold giggled kissing his cheeks.
"That kiss should have been on my lips" Fredrick pouted then Gold smiled wrapping her hands on his shoulders as she pulled him into a short kiss.
AUSTIN POV
Austin felt his blood boil as he watched them kiss, then his hatred for Fredrick grew.
"I must have you Gold, let's see how long you can stick to him when he loses everything. I will ruin you Fredrick and take your beloved from you.
You will pay for what you did to my father but if you think you can be happy, let's see how long your happiness will last" Austin spoke bitterly from his heart with so much hate.

"I have something to tell you," Gold said giggling as she spoke with Ella

"What is it? or are you pregnant? Ella grinned but Gold hit her playfully.

"Geez no, guess some more" Gold said although Ella tried she still couldn't guess correctly.

"Joy was sentenced to death?" Ella said happily, as she hit Gold's shoulders playfully.

"I already told you that," Gold said with a smile

"Well I'm not good at guessing just tell me already" Ella said giving up.

"Well the thing is Fredrick agreed to let you follow us to Abuja" Gold screamed.

"You must be kidding me," Ella asked not wanting to believe.

"Does It look like I'm joking? I'm dead serious" Gold

"Oh my God" Ella screamed happily

hugging Gold tight.
"Am I dreaming or something?" She asked Gold with tears
"No it's real" Gold replied then Ella rushed towards Gold and enveloped her in a tight embrace.
"Thanks, Gold. I love you so much and you are the best friend one can ever ask for" Ella said to Gold as she hugged her again.
"You too, so you will finally get to see your family again"
"Esther is the only family I have and she's the reason why I want to go back"
"What about your mother?" Gold asked.
"She abandoned me and left me in the cruel hands of my foster parent so I don't regard her as my mother Gold" Ella said sadly.
"I bet she regrets it everyday Ella" Gold said to encourage her.
"I don't want to talk about my mother,
hugging Gold tight.
"Am I dreaming or something?" She

let's talk about something else"
"Fine but Fredrick said you will have to come back with us" Gold added.
"That won't be a problem. Moreover I don't intend to stay there for long anyways" Ella replied
"Ok" Gold nodded slightly.
FREDERICK
Frederick sighed tiredly as he sat on his office chair as he just finished his meeting with the board members.
He had to return to work after the court trial but then he saw his brother Ethan walking into his office with a smile on his face.
"Bro you are such a badass genius" he smiled.
"Austin will sure fall into this trap. But bro I'm sure going to miss you" Ethan pouted.
"Don't give me that look, it's just for a few

weeks so while I'm gone, you will be in charge" Fredrick said
"Yeah of course," Ethan said sadly.
"Stop making me feel emotional with that look. I'm not running away" Fredrick rolled his eyes at him.
"You are cold" Ethan muttered.
"Ethan, come on in for a hug" Fredrick said but Ethan looked shocked.
"Frederick, I can't remember the last time we hugged, I guess that was in preschool" Ethan said smiling.
"That's a big lie" Fredrick argued but Ethan insisted
"But it's true"
"Do you want the hug or not?" Frederick asked
"Of course, I do" Ethan grinned and pulled him into a hug and he smiled slightly still hugging him.
"Ethan is really important to me, he's one of reasons, I had to take on my uncle for

the company If I had allowed him to take over, he would have made us miserable and I didn't want that for Ethan nor myself" Fredrick said inwardly.

AERIAL POV

"Sleepyhead wake up," Aerial said as she woke her daughter Queen.

"Mum what is it" Queen mumbled sleep talking.

"Baby wake up" Aerial kept tapping her slightly.

"But I still feel sleepy" she sighed tiredly sitting up on her bed.

"You seem to be forgetting something Queenie Frederick is arriving today" Aerial said with all seriousness to her daughter.

"What? mom, why didn't you wake me earlier?" Queen scolded

"Don't be silly and go take a bath. You are coming with your dad and me to the airport" Aerial said to Queen who

seemed interested
"Yes, mom" she giggled.
"Remember Darling, you have to seduce Fredrick into your bed, get pregnant for him and make sure Gold is kicked out of his life for good.
I want her to feel the pain I felt when Kennedy left me for her mother" Aerial sa, id Queen.
"Don't worry mom, Gold will certainly suffer"
"I know she would, so go freshen up quickly because breakfast is ready"
"Ok mom" Queen smiled and walked into the bathroom.
"I hate you so much Irene and your useless daughter Gold. It feels so good to know that you are dead.
But too bad you won't be able tO watch I make Gold miserable" Aerial said as she smiled and walked out of her daughter's room.

ESTHER

"Honey come to have some more breakfast" Esther's mum reached out to her.

"Mom I'm full already" Esther complained. to her worried mother.

"I know you are not, you are just In a hurry to go see Gold"

"Yeah you caught me on that but I miss her mom. I want to be one of the first persons to see her"

"You shouldn't lie to your mother, of course I would always let you go see old because she's a nice girl and she has been through a lot" Esther's mum spoke compassionately.

"I know that and I'm going to scold her for not telling me about her problems" Esther replied as well

"Well you better get there early so you can scold her Some more" Her mum said then Esther laughed when she said that.

"Thanks, mom," Est h,e r said as she pecked
her cheeks before taking my sling bag
and walked out of the house.
GOLD
Gold sighed tiredly as they walked out of
the airport lounge. They just landed
from one of Fredrick's private jets and the
airport check officer had to screen
their papers.
"Oh my God Gold" Esther ran to hug Gold
and Gold knew she hasn't seen her sister
"I missed you Gold," Esther said touching
and turning her around
"I missed you too bestie" Gold replied
and they slowly pulled out of the hug
and that was when she sighted her sister.
"Emmanuella?" Esther called as her jaw
dropped.
"How? how?" Esther asked confused as
tears rolled freely from her eyes then she
went further and embraced her sister.
"I missed you Ella because I thought you

were dead" Esther stuttered still hugging her sister.
"I will explain everything to you later" Ella assured Esther
"Mom wouldn't stop thinking about you She cried all night for you Ella" Esther said her sister but Ella let out a scoff.
"She was the one who gave me up for adoption so why should she care?" Ella said angrily
"Mom told me you were dead" Esther said
"Yeah, to her I was dead" Ella responded in an upset manner.
"Ella what matters is that you are back now" Esther said and they hugged themselves again.
"So who's that hot guy by your side, your boyfriend?" Esther asked Gold who couldn't help control herself but burst into laughter.
"You haven't changed a bit" Gold said referring to Esther.

"How about an introduction?" Esther requested and Gold obliged
"Frederick this is my friend Esther, and Esther meet my boyfriend, Frederick" Gold said.
"Nice to meet you and thanks for taking care of my naughty friend here" Esther said Fredrick chuckled slightly.
"Esther" Gold called but Esther ignored her and focused on other people
"I agree with her Gold you are naughty" Fredrick winked and Gold bite my lips.
"I can't believe you are taking her side" Gold said to him.
"Speak of the devil" Esther muttered as she sighted Gold's evil stepmom and sister smiling together with her dad.
"What are they doing here?" Gold asked angrily because she detests Queen and her mum a lot and so does Esther.
"Dad" Gold called hugging her father tight.

"Mama, I'm sorry for not being the best father to you"
Mr. Collins apologized to his daughter
"Dad you've already apologized and I have forgiven you" Gold said as she smiled and pulled out of the hug.
"Thanks, Gold and you must be Fredrick, my daughter's boyfriend" Mr. Collins asked referring to Fredrick.
"Yeah I am" Fredrick responded somehow shy
"Thanks for saving my life and thanks for taking care of my daughter" Collins thanked him.
"No need to thank me Sir because Gold is the love of my life and I would do anything for her" Fredrick said but Gold noticed that Queen and her mother were giving her scornful glances but It's normal hence they all hate each other.
"Mama, you are indeed very lucky to have this man in your life, please keep him ok?" Mr. Collins said to his daughter.

"Mama, I'm sorry for not being the best father to you"
Mr. Collins apologized to his daughter
"Dad you've already apologized and I have forgiven you" Gold said as she smiled and pulled out of the hug.
"Thanks, Gold and you must be Fredrick, my daughter's boyfriend" Mr. Collins asked referring to Fredrick.
"Yeah I am" Fredrick responded somehow shy
"Thanks for saving my life and thanks for taking care of my daughter" Collins thanked him.
"No need to thank me Sir because Gold is the love of my life and I would do anything for her" Fredrick said but Gold noticed that Queen and her mother were giving her scornful glances but It's normal hence they all hate each other.
"Mama, you are indeed very lucky to have this man in your life, please keep him ok?" Mr. Collins said to his daughter.

Gold muttered inwardly.
"If I can remember vividly, I didn't do anything wrong. I only said the truth, you are a witch Aeriel and that's the truth. I thought you never really liked me, so what the hell are you doing here with your dumb ass daughter dressed like a prostitute?" Gold said angrily.
"Mom she just called me a prostitute" Queen complained
"How dare you?" Ariel proceed to slap Gold but Fredrick held her hand and pushed it away.
"She's my girlfriend and I forbid you from laying a finger on her" Fredrick told her sternly and Gold smiled.
"But ....but you heard what she said" Ariel referred to Fredrick
"I don't care but don't try to hurt my girlfriend. You should ask Ela what I did to those who tried to touch her. Come on baby, let's go" Fredrick said to Gold who smiled broadly as they walked away.
AERIAL

"Collins, did you see that? See how rude and insolent your daughter has become, just because she has a rich guy as a boyfriend" Aerial yelled.
"What do you want me to do?" Collins yelled.
"Scold her of course" Aerial replied angrily
"Aerial I'm so sick and tired of you. I asked you before we left home why Queen was dressed like this but you told me to mind my business.
Now it's obvious you brought her here to seduce Fredrick and you are jealous of Gold's progress.
Can't you see how you are both embarrassed yourselves, he didn't even spare you a look" Collins said angrily.
"Collins so you're taking her side" Aerial asked
"Daddy how can Gold get so lucky, she doesn't deserve to be happy" Queen Screamed in tears.

"Aerial see what you are teaching your daughter. How can you get so greedy and inconsiderate? Can you go through all that Gold has been through and stand here?
No, you can't because you are weak and selfish Queen and It was because of you Aerial that I didn't take responsibility of my child when her mum died.
She was rapped by that pig, abused, beaten, do you even know what she went through in Lagos and now that someone good came her way, you try to take what is not yours.
This should be the very last time this nonsense repeats itself" Collins yell in anger at Queen and Aerial
"Collins has never spoken this way to me before but he. just did and it means only one thing that Gold must have brainwashed him" Aerial thought inwardly.
"How dare you yell at me, Collins? because of that mistake of a daughter?"

Aerial asked angrily.
"Listen to me, Gold is not a mistake because I married her mother and she was born out of love.
You are the mistake Aerial, you ruined the relationship I had with Irene with your useless child.
You made it clear before that you didn't want me, you wanted a rich guy who would take care of your needs. But when you left, Irene helped me build back my life and we were happy having Gold as our only child until you came along with Queen claiming that she was my child.
You destroyed my family and drugged me to sign the divorce papers, you made me abandon my child. What was I thinking marrying a devil like you?"
Collins said angrily regretting everything he ever had with Aerial.
"Collins, you only realize now that I'm a the devil and to think that you want to re Marrying Irene makes me laugh. But too bad, she's in the grave and you have just

me" Aerial smiled at Collins deceptively.
"You witch, I'm out of here," Collins said and walked to where they parked the car with Queen and Aerial following closely behind.
"Collins, Collins, I'm talking to you" Aerial called but Collins ignored her and got into the car shutting the door. She tried to open the door but it didn't open.

To be continued to the conclusion part

www.ingramcontent.com/pod-product-compliance
Lightning Source LLC
LaVergne TN
LVHW012058160826
845678LV00014B/2872

* 9 7 9 8 3 5 1 5 9 6 3 7 2 *